PRECAUTIONS TO AVOID POSSIBLE EXPOSURE TO EXCESSIVE MICROWAVE ENERGY

1. **Do Not Attempt** to operate the oven with the door open since open-door operation can result in harmful exposure to microwave energy. It is important not to defeat or tamper with the safety interlocks.

2. **Do Not Place** any object between the oven front face and the door or allow soil or cleaner residue to accumulate on sealing surfaces.

3. **Do Not Operate** the oven if it is damaged. It is particularly important that the oven door close properly and that there is no damage to the (1) door (bent), (2) hinges and latches (broken or loosened), (3) door seals and sealing surfaces.

4. **The Oven Shoud not** be adjusted or repaired by anyone except properly qualified service personnel.

Contents

4 Heating or Reheating Chart

1. Directions below are for reheating already-cooked foods at refrigerator or room temperature. Use microwave oven safe containers.
2. Cover most foods (see tips) for fastest heating. Exceptions are rare or medium meats, some sandwiches, griddle foods like pancakes and baked foods.
3. Where appropriate, use the automatic food temperature control for accurate heating. Place probe horizontally so tip is in center of food about 1-in. from top surface. Bubbling around edges of dish is normal, since center is last to heat. Suggested serving temperatures are given for most foods. Young children usually prefer cooler food, generally about 20° lower. Adjust temperatures to your personal taste. Stir foods before serving.
4. Be sure foods are heated through before serving. Steaming or bubbling around edges does not necessarily mean food is heated throughout. As a general rule, hot foods produce an area warm to the touch in center of underside of dish.

ITEM	Amount	Suggested Serving Temp.	Power Level	Approximate Time, Min.
Appetizers				
Saucy: such as meatballs, riblets, cocktail	1 to 2 servings	150°	HI (10)	1 to 3
franks, etc.	3 to 4 servings	150°	HI (10)	3½ to 5
½ cup/serving				
Dips: cream or process cheese	½ cup	130°	Med-HI (7)	1½ to 2
	1 cup	130°	Med-HI (5)	3 to 5
Pastry bites: small pizzas, egg rolls, etc.	2 to 4 servings		HI (10)	½ to 1½

Tip: Cover saucy appetizers with wax paper. Cover dips with plastic wrap. Do not cover pastry bites, so that they will crisp.

ITEM	Amount	Suggested Serving Temp.	Power Level	Approximate Time, Min.
Plate of Leftovers				
Meat plus 2 vegetables	1 plate	150° to 160°	HI (10)	2 to 3

Tip: Probe works well in saucy dishes or vegetables (use in largest serving) but not in meat slices. Cover plate of food with waxed paper or plastic wrap.)

ITEM	Amount	Suggested Serving Temp.	Power Level	Approximate Time, Min.
Meats and Main Dishes				
Saucy Main Dishes: chop suey, spaghetti,	1 to 2 servings	150° to 160°	HI (10)	3 to 5
creamed chicken, chili, stew, macaroni and	3 to 4 servings	150° to 160°	HI (10)	8 to 12
cheese, etc.	1 can 16-oz.	150° to 160°	HI (10)	4½ to 6
¾ to 1 cup/serving				
Thinly sliced roasted meat:				
Rare beef roast, minimum time; Medium Rare,	1 to 2 servings		Med-HI (7)	1 to 2
maximum time	3 to 4 servings		Med-HI (7)	2 to 3
3 to 4-oz./serving				
Well done: beef, pork, ham, poultry, etc.	1 to 2 servings		Med-HI (7)	1 to 2
	3 to 4 servings		Med-HI (7)	3 to 4
Steaks, chops, ribs, other meat pieces:				
Rare beef steak	1 to 2 servings	130°	Med-HI (7)	2 to 3
	3 to 4 servings	130°	Med-HI (7)	4 to 6
Well done beef, chops, ribs, etc.	1 to 2 servings	150°	Med-HI (7)	2 to 3
	3 to 4 servings	150°	Med-HI (7)	4 to 6
Hamburgers or meat loaf	1 to 2 servings		HI (10)	1 to 2
4-oz./serving	3 to 4 servings		HI (10)	2 to 3
Chicken pieces	1 to 2 pieces		HI (10)	½ to 1
	3 to 4 pieces		HI (10)	1 to 2
Hot Dogs and sausages	1 to 2		HI (10)	½ to 1
	3 to 4		HI (10)	1 to 2
Rice and pasta	1 to 2 servings	150°	HI (10)	1 to 2
⅔ to ¾ cup/serving				
Topped or mixed with sauce	1 to 2 servings	150° to 160°	HI (10)	1 to 3
⅔ to ¾ cup/serving	3 to 4 servings	150° to 160°	HI (10)	4 to 6

Tip: Cover saucy main dishes with plastic wrap. Cover other main dishes and meats with wax paper. Do not cover rare or medium rare meats.

ITEM	Amount	Suggested Serving Temp.	Power Level	Approximate Time, Min.
Sandwiches & Soups				
Moist filling: Sloppy Joes, barbecue, ham salad, etc. in bun	1 to 2 servings		Med-HI (7)	1 to 2
⅓ cup/serving	3 to 4 servings		Med-HI (7)	2½ to 3
Thick meat-cheese filling; with firm bread	1 to 2 servings		Med-HI (7)	½ to 1
	3 to 4 servings		Med-HI (7)	1½ to 2
Soup				
Water based	1 to 2 servings	150° to 170°	HI (10)	2 to 4
1 cup/serving	3 to 4 servings	150° to 170°	HI (10)	5 to 9
	1 can 10-oz.	150° to 170°	HI (10)	4 to 5
Milk based	1 to 2 servings	140°	Med-HI (7)	3 to 5
1 cup/serving	3 to 4 servings	140°	Med-HI (7)	6 to 8
	1 can 10-oz.	140°	Med-HI (7)	5 to 6

Tip: Use paper towel or napkin to cover sandwiches. Cover soups with wax paper or plastic wrap.

ITEM	Amount	Suggested Serving Temp.	Power Level	Approximate Time, Min.
Vegetables				
Small pieces: peas, beans, corn, etc.	1 to 2 servings	150° to 160°	HI (10)	1 to 3
½ cup/serving	3 to 4 servings	150° to 160°	HI (10)	3 to 4
	1 can 16-oz.	150° to 160°	HI (10)	3½ to 4½
Large pieces or whole: asparagus spears, corn on the cob, etc.	1 to 2 servings		HI (10)	1½ to 3
	3 to 4 servings		HI (10)	2 to 4
	1 can 16-oz.		HI (10)	4 to 5
Mashed	1 to 2 servings	150° to 160°	HI (10)	2 to 3
½ cup/serving	3 to 4 servings	150° to 160°	HI (10)	3 to 5

Tip: Cover vegetables for most even heating.

ITEM	Amount	Suggested Serving Temp.	Power Level	Approximate Time, Min.
Sauces				
Dessert: chocolate, butterscotch	½ cup	125°	HI (10)	½ to 1½
	1 cup	125°	HI (10)	1½ to 2
Meat or main dish: chunky type, giblet gravy, spaghetti sauce, etc.	½ cup	150° to 160°	HI (10)	1½ to 2½
	1 cup	150° to 160°	HI (10)	2½ to 3
	1 can 16-oz.	150° to 160°	HI (10)	4 to 5
Creamy type	½ cup	140° to 150°	HI (10)	1 to 1½
	1 cup	140° to 150°	HI (10)	1½ to 2

Tip: Cover food to prevent spatter.

ITEM	Amount	Suggested Serving Temp.	Power Level	Approximate Time, Min.
Bakery Foods				
Cake, coffee cake, doughnuts, sweet rolls, nut or fruit bread	1 piece		Low (3)	½ to 1
	2 pieces		Low (3)	1½ to 2
	4 pieces		Low (3)	1½ to 2½
	9-in. cake or 12 rolls or doughnuts		Low (3)	2 to 3
Dinner rolls, muffins	1		Med (5)	¼ to ½
	2		Med (5)	½ to ¾
	4		Med (5)	½ to 1
	6 to 8		Med (5)	¾ to 1
Pie: fruit, nut or custard	1 slice		HI (10)	½ to ¾
⅛ of 9-in. pie=1 slice	2 slices		HI (10)	1 to 1½
(use minimum time for custard)	4 slices		Med-HI (7)	2½ to 3
	9-in. pie		Med-HI (7)	3 to 5

ITEM	Amount	Suggested Serving Temp.	Power Level	Approximate Time, Min.
Griddle Foods				
Pancakes, French Toast or Waffles (3"×4")				
Plain, no topping	2 or 3 pieces		HI (10)	½ to 1
Syrup & butter	2 or 3 pieces		HI (10)	1 to 1¼
With 2 sausage patties (cooked)	2 or 3 pieces		HI (10)	1¼ to 1½

ITEM	Amount	Suggested Serving Temp.	Power Level	Approximate Time, Min.
Beverages				
Coffee, tea, cider	1 to 2 cups	160° to 170°	HI (10)	2 to 3
Other water based	3 to 4 cups	160° to 170°	HI (10)	4 to 6
Cocoa, other milk based	1 to 2 cups	140°	Med-HI (7)	3 to 5
	3 to 4 cups	140°	Med-HI (7)	6 to 8

Tip: Do not cover bakery foods, griddle foods (pancakes, etc.) or beverages.

6 Defrosting Chart

1. Food packaged in all-paper or plastic packages may be defrosted without unwrapping. If food is foil wrapped, remove foil and place food in cooking dish for defrosting.
2. After first half of cooking time, unwrap package and check food. Turn food over, if necessary; break apart or separate food if possible. On very large foods like turkey, some shielding of thin wing or leg areas may be necessary.
3. Be sure large meats are completely defrosted (or, on roasts allow extra microwaving time). Turkeys may be placed under running water until giblets can be removed.
4. When defrosted, food should be cool but softened in all areas. If still slightly icy, return to microwave oven very briefly, or let stand a few minutes.

POWER LEVEL: **Defrost (3)**

FOOD	First Half Time, Min.	Second Half Time, Min.	Comments
Meat			
Bacon (12 to 16 oz.)	1½	1½ to 3½	Place unopened package in oven. After half of time, turn package over and rotate ¼ turn. Let stand 5 minutes.
Franks (1-lb.)	4 to 5	none	Place unopened package in oven. Microwave just until franks can be separated.
Ground: beef & pork (1-lb.)	4	3 to 4	Turn over after first 4 minutes.
(2-lbs.)	6	5 to 6	Scrape off softened meat after second half of time. Set aside. Break up remaining block, microwave 3 to 4 minutes more.
(5-lbs.)	12	12 to 14	Scrape off softened meat after second half of time. Set aside. Break up remaining block, microwave 11 to 12 minutes more.
Roast: Beef	3 to 4 per lb.	3 to 4 per lb.	Place unwrapped roast in oven. After half of time turn roast over. Defrost for second half of time. Let stand for 30 minutes.
Roast: Pork	4 to 5 per lb.	4 to 5 per lb.	Place wrapped package in oven fat side down. Turn over after first half of time.
Spareribs, pork (1 pkg.)	3 to 4 per lb.	3 to 4 per lb.	Place wrapped package in microwave safe dish. After first half of time, turn package over. Continue defrosting. Separate pieces and let stand to complete defrosting.
Steaks, chops & cutlets; beef, lamb, pork & veal	2 to 4 per lb.	2 to 4½ per lb.	Place wrapped package in oven in microwave safe dish. Turn over after first half of time. After second half of time, separate pieces with table knife, let stand to complete defrosting.
Sausage, bulk (1-lb. tray)	2	2 to 4	Remove metal ends. Turn over after first 2½ minutes. Let stand 5 minutes.
(1-lb. roll)	2	2 to 3	
Sausage, link (1 to 1½-lb.)	2	1½ to 2½	
Sausage, patties (12-oz. pkg.)	1	1 to 2	
Poultry			
Chicken, broiler-fryer, cut up (2½ to 3½-lb.)	6 to 7	6 to 7	Place wrapped chicken in oven. Unwrap and turn over after half of time. After second half of time, separate pieces and place in cooking dish. Defrost 2 to 4 minutes more, if necessary.
Whole (2½ to 3½-lb.)	6 to 8	6 to 8	Place wrapped chicken in oven. After ¼ of time turn over chicken. After half of time, unwrap and place in microwave safe dish and shield warm areas with foil. After ¾ time, turn chicken over. Let stand to complete defrosting.
Cornish hen	3 to 4 per lb.	3 to 4 per lb.	Place wrapped package in oven breast side down. Turn package over after first half of time. Run under cool water to complete defrosting.
Ducking	3 to 4 per lb.	3 to 4 per lb.	Place wrapped duckling in oven. After first ¼ of time, unwrap and turn over into cooking dish. Shield warm areas with foil. After ¾ time, turn over. Let stand to complete defrosting.
Turkey	Total 3 to 4 per lb.		Place unwrapped turkey breast side up in microwave safe dish. Defrost ⅓ time. Turn turkey on its side and defrost for second ⅓ of time. Unwrap and shield legs, wings, and any other warm areas. Turn turkey breast side down and continue defrosting. Let soak in cool water or refrigerate overnight to complete defrosting.

POWER LEVEL: **Defrost (3)**

FOOD	First Half Time, Min.	Second Half Time, Min.	Comments
Fish & Seafood			
Fillets (1-lb.)	4	4 to 6	Place unopened package in oven. (If fish is frozen in water, place in cooking dish.) Turn package over after first half of time. After second half of time, hold under cold water separate.
Steaks (6-oz.)	2 to 3	1 to 2	
Whole fish (8 to 10-oz.)	3	2 to 4	Place fish in cooking dish. Turn over after first half of time. After second half of time, rinse cavity with cold water to complete defrosting.
Shellfish, small pieces (1-lb.)	4 to 4½	4 to 4½	Spread shellfish in single layer in baking dish.
Shellfish, blocks Crab meat (6-oz. pkg.)	4 to 5	none	Place block in casserole.
Oysters (10-oz. can)	8 to 10	none	Place block in casserole. Break up with fork after first half of time.
Scallops (1-lb. pkg.)	3 to 4	3 to 4	Place unopened package in oven. Turn over after ½ time.
Shellfish, large:			
Crab legs—1 to 2 (8 to 10-oz.)	3 to 4	3 to 4	Place in microwave safe dish. Rearrange after ½ time.
Lobster tails—1 to 2 (6 to 9-oz.)	6 to 8	none	Place in microwave safe dish.
Whole lobster or crab (1½-lb.)	7 to 8	7 to 8	Place in microwave safe dish with light underside down. Turn over after first half of time.
Breads, Cakes			
Bread or buns (1-lb.)	3 to 4	none	Turn over after ½ time.
Heat & serve rolls (7-oz. pkg.)	2 to 3	none	
Coffee Cake (11 to 14¾-oz.)	2½ to 3	none	
Coffee ring (10-oz. pkg.)	3 to 5	none	Rotate ½ turn after half of time.
Sweet rolls (8¾ to 12-oz.)	3 to 6	none	Rotate ½ turn after half of time.
Doughnuts (1 to 3)	½ to 2	none	
Doughnuts, glazed (1 box of 12)	3 to 4	none	
French Toast (2 slices)	3 to 3½	none	
Cake, frosted 2 to 3 layer (17-oz.)	2½ to 3	none	
Cake, filled or topped 1 layer (12½ to 16-oz.)	2½ to 3	none	
Pound cake (11¼-oz.)	2	none	Remove from foil tray.
Cheesecake, plain or fruit top (17 to 19-oz.)	5 to 6	none	
Crunch cakes & cupcakes	½ to 1 each	none	
Fruit or nut pie (8-in.)	4 to 7	none	Remove from foil tray.
Cream or custard pie (14-oz.)	3 to 4	none	Remove from foil tray.
Fruit			
Fresh (10 to 16-oz.)	5 to 8	none	Place package in oven. Remove foil or metal. After minimum time, break up with fork. Repeat if necessary.
Plastic pouch—1 to 2 (10-oz. pkg.)	6 to 9	none	Slit package. Place package in oven. Flex package once.

8 Convenience Food Chart

1. Most convenience foods can be reheated by microwave only, since they are already cooked. Always use microwave safe utensils (glass or plastic). For foods needing browning or crisping, conventional baking is recommended.
2. Remove food from foil containers over ¾-in. high and place in microwave safe container.
3. Amounts can be increased. To cook multiple packages, add times togehter.

FOOD	Container	Cover	Power Level	Microwave Time	Comments
Appetizers & Snacks					
Pastry Bites (3 to 4 oz.)	Microwave safe dish	No	HI (10)	1 to 2 min.	
Frozen prepared sandwiches	Paper towel	No	HI (10)	1 to 2 min. per sandwich	Remove from foil package and wrap in paper towel. Rotate ½ turn after half of time.
Popcorn	Microwave bag	No	HI (10)	3 to 5 min.	Follow package directions.
Eggs & Cheese					
Scrambled egg substitute (8 oz. carton)	Microwave safe dish	No	HI (10)	1½ to 2½ min.	Microwave about ½ minute per ¼ cup mixture. Stir after half of time.
Cheese souffle (12 oz.)	Microwave safe 8" pie plate and custard cups	No	Defrost (3) Med-HI (7)	5 to 7 min. 5 to 9 min.	To Defrost: Place in 8-in. pie plate. Stir twice. To Cook: Divide between 3 or 4 buttered custard cups 6 or 7-oz. Rearrange after 5 minutes. Souffles are done when center is set.
Scrambled eggs Breakfast (6¼-oz.) with sausage and hash brown potatoes	Package paper tray	Package cover	HI (10)	3½ to 4 min.	Remove paper tray from carton, turn back oven film to expose potatoes.
Fish & Shellfish					
Crab or shrimp newburg (6½-oz.)	Package pouch	No	HI (10)	4 to 5 min.	Puncture pouch with fork to vent.
Fish & chips (5 to 14-oz.)	Package tray	No	HI (10)	3 to 4 min.	Remove foil cover. Return tray to carton or distribute evenly on microwave safe dish.
Deviled crab (6-oz.)	Microwave safe dish	No	HI (10)	2 to 4 min.	
Breaded fish (5 to 10 oz.) (14 to 16-oz.) (23 to 25-oz.)	Microwave safe dish	No	HI (10)	3 to 4 min. 5 to 6 min. 7 to 9 min.	Distribute evenly on microwave safe dish.
Meat					
Frozen meats (5 to 8 oz.) (10 to 16-oz.) (16 to 32-oz.)	Microwave safe dish or pouch	No	HI (10)	4 to 6 min. 7 to 11 min. 12 to 18 min.	If pouch package is used puncture with fork to vent.
Dry mixes (hamburger added)	Microwave safe casserole		HI (10)	10 to 16 min.	Add cooked, drained hamburger.
T.V. dinners (6 to 11½-oz.) (12 to 20-oz.)	Package tray and carton	Carton	HI (10)	5 to 8 min. 6 to 11 min.	Remove foil cover, replace in carton. (Any batter foods should be removed before cooking.)
Pasta, Rice					
Canned spaghetti, etc.	Microwave safe dish	Lid or plastic wrap	HI (10)	2 to 4 min.	Stir before serving.
Frozen rice in pouch (10-oz.)	Pouch		HI (10)	4 to 6 min.	Puncture pouch with fork to vent.
Frozen macaroni & cheese spaghetti (8 to 14-oz.)	Microwave safe dish	Lid or plastic wrap	HI (10)	6 to 9 min.	Stir before serving.
Frozen Lasagna (21-oz.)	Microwave safe dish	Wax paper or plastic wrap	HI (10)	12 to 14 min.	

FOOD	Container	Cover	Power Level	Microwave Time	Comments
Poultry					
Canned (7½ to 10½-oz.)	Microwave safe dish	Lid or plastic wrap	HI (10)	2 to 3 min.	Place in microwave safe dish. Cover; stir after half time.
(14 to 24-oz.)			HI (10)	4 to 6 min.	
Frozen Pouch (5 to 6½-oz.)			HI (10)	2½ to 3½ min.	Slit pouch before microwaving.
Main dish (12 to 17-oz. pkg.)	Microwave safe dish	No	HI (10)	7 to 9 min.	Stir after half of time.
Fried chicken 2-pieces	Microwave safe dish	No	HI (10)	2 to 4 min.	If label does not state "fully cooked", check for doneness.
1-lb., 6 pieces			HI (10)	5½ to 7 min.	
2-lbs., 8 to 10 pieces			HI (10)	7 to 9 min.	
Sauces, Gravies					
Canned (10 to 16-oz.)	Microwave safe dish	Lid or plastic wrap	HI (10)	2 to 4 min.	
(32-oz.)				4 to 6 min.	
Vegetables					
Frozen breaded (7-oz.)	Microwave safe dish	No	HI (10)	2 to 4 min.	Place on microwave trivet or dish.
Canned (8 to 9-oz.)	Microwave safe dish	Lid or plastic wrap	HI (10)	1 to 3 min.	Place vegetables in microwave safe dish. Add ½ cup liquid or liquid from can. Cover. (Or use temperature probe set to 150°.)
(15 to 17-oz.)			HI (10)	3 to 4½ min.	
(28 to 32-oz.)			HI (10)	5 to 7 min.	
Instant mashed potatoes:	Microwave safe dish	Lid or plastic wrap			Use container size and amounts of water, milk, butter and salt on package. Cover. After heating, briskly stir in potatoes, adding extra 1 to 2 tablespoons dry mix.
2 to 6 servings			HI (10)	3 to 4 min.	
8 to 12 servings			HI (10)	5 to 8 min.	
Souffle, frozen (12-oz. pkg.)	Microwave safe pie plate	No	HI (10)	5 to 7 min.	Stir after half of time.
Potatoes: baked, stuffed, frozen	Microwave safe dish	Wax paper			Check to see that potatoes are NOT IN FOIL. Rotate ½ turn after half of time.
1 to 2			HI (10)	4 to 6 min.	
3 to 4			HI (10)	6 to 8 min.	

10 Meats

1. Always use microwave-safe dish, plastic or glass.
2. Standing time: Allow about 10 minutes standing time for most roasts, before carving.

FOOD	Container	Cover	Power Level & Time (or Internal Temp.)		Comments
Beef Ground Crumbled (for casseroles or soup)	Casserole	No	HI (10)	1 lb.: 5 to 6 min. 1½ lb.: 7 to 9 min.	Add sauce or casserole ingredients and finish. To cook frozen block, microwave 10 to 15 minutes breaking up and stirring every 5 minutes.
Meatballs	Round or oblong dish	Wax paper	HI (10)	1 lb.: 6 to 8 min. 2 lb.: 10 to 14 min.	Round dish: arrange ¾ to 1-in. apart in circle around edge of dish. Oblong dish: arrange ¾ to 1-in. aprart.
Patties	Oblong glass dish (with trivet if desired) ceramic dinner plate (For 1 or 2 patties use paper plate lined with double thickness paper towels.)	Wax paper	HI (10)	4 patties/lb. 1 to 2 patties: 2 to 4 min. 3 to 4 patties: 4 to 6 min.	Cover with wax paper or cook uncovered and turn patties over after ½ of time. If desired, add browning sauce or agent.
Meat loaf	Pie plate or loaf dish	Plastic wrap	Med-HI (7)	Round loaf: 21 to 23 min.	Let stand 10 minutes after cooking.
			Med (5) or cook to 170°	Loaf shape: 29 to 32 min.	
Roasts Pot roasts (3 to 5-lb.)	Oblong dish or casserole	Lid or plastic wrap	Med (5)	1 to 1½-hrs.	Brush with browning sauce and add ½ cup water. Turn over after half of time. Add vegetables if desired after half of time. Recover and finish cooking.
Simmered beef, corned beef or brisket (2½ to 3-lb.)	Casserole	Lid or plastic wrap	Low (3)	2 to 2¼-hrs.	Add 1 cup water per lb. meat. Turn over after half of time. Let meat stand in broth at least 10 minutes after cooking. For boiled dinner, remove meat, cook vegetables in broth.
Tender roasts (rib, high quality rump, sirloin tip)	Oblong dish and trivet	Wax paper	Med (5)	**Min. per lb.** **Internal Temp.**	Temperature probe cooking yields most accurate results. Let meat stand 10 to 15 minutes before carving. If desired, brush with browning sauce or agent before cooking.
				Rare 10 to 12 120° to 125° Medium 13 to 15 130° to 140° Well 15 to 17 155° to 165°	
PORK Bacon	Microwave safe plate or oblong dish	Paper towel	HI (10)	Per slice: ¾ to 1 min. 1 lb.: 11 to 14 min. total	Arrange in single layer on paper towels or on trivet set in dish. Layer many slices between layers of paper towels in oblong dish.
Pork sausage (raw)	Microwave safe utensil	Wax paper	HI (10)	½ lb.: 4 patties ½ to ¾ min. per patty.	Arrange in single layer.
Pork link sausage (raw)	Microwave safe utensil	Wax paper	HI (10)	½ to ¾ min. per link	Arrange in single layer.
Canadian bacon	Microwave safe utensil	Wax paper	HI (10)	2 slices ¾ to 1¼ min. 4 slices 1½ to 2 min. 6 slices 2 to 2½ min.	Arrange in single layer.
Pork chops (1-in. thick)	Microwave safe utensil	Plastic wrap	Med (5)	2: 11 to 13 min. 3: 14 to 17 min. 4: 20 to 25 min. 6: 27 to 31 min.	Brush with barbecue sauce or browning agent, if desired. Let stand covered 5 to 10 minutes before serving.

FOOD	Container	Cover	Power Level & Time (or Internal Temp.)		Comments
Pork roast	Oblong glass baking dish	Cooking bag method	Med (5)	15 to 17 min. per lb. Or microwave to 170° internal temp.	Place roast in a cooking bag without water. Tie end of bag securely. Make small slit near closure. Do not use metal twist ties. Or if preferred, place fat side up on trivet in dish. Add water to dish and cover with wax paper. Microwave at Med (5) 17 to 19 min. per lb.
Spare ribs	3-qt. oblong glass baking dish or casserole	Plastic wrap or cover	Med (5)	25 to 30 min. per lb.	Add ⅔ cup water per lb. spare ribs. Turn over or rearrange after half of minimum time. After minimum time, drain liquid and add barbecue sauce; microwave few minutes to finish.
Ham roast	2 or 3-qt. oblong glass baking dish	Plastic wrap	Med (5) Precooked or Canned	**Min. per lb.** / **Internal Temp.** 11 to 13 / 115°	Shield top edge of ham with 1½-in. strip of foil. After cooking period let ham stand 10 minutes before carving.
Ham loaf	1½-qt. oblong glass baking dish	Plastic wrap	Med-HI (7) (or microwave to internal temp of 170°)	19 to 21 min.	Shape into oval loaf with rounded corners. Remove loaf from oven, let stand 5 minutes before serving. If a glaze is desired, spoon pineapple or apricot preserves over cooked ham loaf a few minutes before serving.
Ham slices & steaks	2-qt. oblong glass baking dish	Wax paper	Med-HI (7)	18 to 22 min.	Turn over at half time.
LAMB Chops	2-qt. oblong glass baking dish	No	HI (10)	4 chops: 5 to 7 min.	Turn meat at half of time.
Roast (Leg or shoulder)	3-qt. oblong glass baking dish	Wax paper	Med (5) (Or cook to 180° for well-done)	15 to 17 min. per lb.	Turn roast over after half of time. Let roast stand 10 minutes before carving. When using temperature probe, insert so tip is not in bone or fat.
VEAL Chops	See lamb chops above.				
Roast (shoulder)	2-qt. oblong glass baking dish and trivet	Wax paper	Med (5) (Or cook to 155°)	15 to 17 min. per lb.	Place on trivet. Cover loosely with wax paper. Turn over after half of cooking time. Let roast stand 10 minutes before carving. Slice thinly.

12 Poultry

1. Use microwave trivet for chicken and other small poultry, but avoid trivet for cooking turkey.
2. Let chicken and other small poultry stand after microwaving for up to 10 minutes. Turkey should be allowed to stand 20 minutes.

FOOD	Container	Cover	Power Level & Time (or Internal Temp.)		Comments
CHICKEN					
Pieces	Plate or oblong dish	Wax paper	HI (10)	Per piece: 2 to 3 min. Whole chicken (8 pieces); 12 to 14 min. total	Brush with browning agent if desired. Arrange in single layer in cooking dish so thickest meaty pieces are to outside edges of dish.
Whole uncut (stuffed or unstuffed)	2-qt. oblong glass baking dish	Oven-proof cooking bag	Med-HI (7) (Or cook to 190° internal temp.)	7 to 9 min. per lb.	Brush with browning agent if desired. Add ⅓ cup water to cooking bag. Slit bag near closure to vent. Do not use metal tie on bag. Cook breast side up. Or, place chicken breast down on trivet in dish and cover with wax paper. Microwave at Med-HI (7) 9 to 10 minutes per lb., turning over and recovering after half of time.
Stewing	Large casserole	Lid or plastic wrap	HI (10) Med (5)	15 min. Then 20 to 22 min. per lb.	Add 1 cup water per lb. chicken, along with 1 to 2 cups onions, celery or carrots as desired. Turn chicken over every 30 minutes.
CORNISH HENS					
Whole (stuffed or unstuffed)	2-qt. oblong glass baking dish and trivet	Wax paper	HI (10)	4 to 6 min. per lb.	
Halves	2-qt. oblong glass baking dish	Wax paper	HI (10)	6 to 8 min. per lb.	Arrange skin side up in dish.
DUCKLING	2-qt. oblong glass baking dish and trivet	Wax paper	HI (10)	6 to 8 min. per lb.	Shield bottom of legs. Microwave breast side up. Brush with browning sauce. Or do not apply browning sauce and broil top surface of cooked bird until brown and crisp.
TURKEY	3-qt. oblong glass baking dish		Med (5)	11 to 13 min. per lb.	Brush with browning agent if desired. Add ½ cup water to cooking bag. Slit bag near closure to vent. Do not use metal tie on bag. Cook breast side up. Or, place turkey breast up on trivet in dish and cover with wax paper. Microwave at Med (5) 18 to 20 minutes per lb. Remove wax paper, baste and turn ½ turn after half of time.

Breads

1. Crust on breads will be soft, outside color of foods will be same as color of batter (outsides will not brown). If desired, sprinkle top of batter with cinnamon-sugar mixture, chopped nuts or other topping for brown color. Or, increase brown color on upside down breads by lining dish before microwaving with brown sugar caramel mixture, or savory topping like crushed canned French fried onion rings.

FOOD	Container	Cover	Power Level	Microwave Time		Comments
Coffee Cakes From refrigerated biscuits	8-in. tube dish*	No	Med-HI (7)	6 to 8 min.		Arrange biscuits over brown sugar-butter topping before microwaving. Rotate ½ turn after 3 minutes. Invert to serve.
Corn Bread	8–9-in. tube dish*	No	Med (5)	10 to 12 min.		For flavorful browned topping sprinkle cooking dish with finely chopped canned French fried onions before microwaving. Turn out of pan upside down to serve.
Muffins	Paper-lined muffin cups (Do not use foil liners)	No	Med-HI (7) 1 Muffin: 2 to 4: 5 to 6:	½ to 1 min. 1 to 1½ min. 1½ to 3 min.		Use microwave muffin container or homemade muffin cups made by cutting down hot paper drink cups.
Quick Breads, Loaf	Glass loaf dish	No	Med-HI (7)	9 to 12 min.		When done, toothpick inserted in center will come out clean. Let stand 15 min. before turning out of dish. Cool.

*If tube dish is unavailable, microwave in 8" round dish with drinking glass placed open-side-up in center.

Eggs and Cheese

1. Prepare eggs many ways in the microwave oven, see below. Always pierce whole yolks before microwaving to prevent bursting.
2. Never hard cook eggs in the shell, and do not reheat in-shell hard cooked eggs. They could explode.
3. Cook eggs just until set, they are delicate and can toughen if overcooked.

FOOD	Container	Cover	Power Level	Microwave Time	Comments
EGGS					
Scrambled	Glass measuring cup or casserole	No	HI (10)	¾ to 1 min. per egg	Melt 1 teaspoon butter per egg in dish. Scramble the eggs with the butter and 1 tablespoon milk per egg. Place in oven and microwave for ½ of total time. Stir set portions from the outside to the center. Continue microwaving. Allow to stand 1 or 2 minutes to set eggs.
Basic eggs	Buttered custard cup	Plastic wrap	Med (5)	¾ to 1 min. per egg	Puncture membrane of yolk to prevent bursting.
Poached eggs	1½-qt. casserole	Casserole cover	HI (10) Med (5)	5 to 6 min. Boil 2 cups water ¾ to 1 min. per egg	Heat 2 cups hot tap water 5 to 6 minutes on HI (10). Break eggs onto plate, puncture membrane. Swirl boiling water with spoon, slip in eggs gently. Cover, microwave at Medium (5). Let stand in water a few minutes.
Omelet	9" pie plate	No	HI (10) Med (5)	Melt butter 1 min. 7 to 10 min.	Sprinkle cheese over omelet. Microwave ½ to 1 minute until cheese is slightly melted. See recipe page 62.
CHEESE					
Fondue	Microwave safe 2-qt. casserole	Cover or plastic wrap	HI (10) Med (5)	To heat wine 4 min. 4 to 5 min.	Use 1 cup wine and 3 tablespoons flour per lb. of shredded cheese. Add cheese, flour and seasonings to hot wine and microwave at Med (5) stirring every 2 minutes until melted.

Fish and Seafood

1. Fish is done when it flakes easily with a fork. Center may still be slightly translucent, but will continue cooking as fish stands a few minutes after cooking.
2. Cook fish with or without sauce. A tight cover steams fish, or use a lighter cover of wax paper or paper towel for less steaming.
3. Do not overcook fish. Check at minimum time.

FOOD	Container	Cover	Power Level & Time (or Internal Temp.)		Comments
FISH					
Fillets or steaks 1 lb.	2-qt. oblong glass baking dish	Wax paper or plastic wrap	HI (10)	6 to 8 min.	Microwave until fish flakes easily.
Whole fish	2 or 3-qt. oblong glass baking dish	Plastic wrap	HI (10) (or cook to internal temp. of 150°)	5 to 7 min. per lb.	Shield head and thin part of tail with aluminum foil.
Clams, 6	Pie plate or shallow dish	Plastic wrap	HI (10)	3 to 5 min.	
Shrimp—1-lb. (peeled)	Pie plate or shallow dish	Plastic wrap	HI (10)	5 to 6 min.	Rearrange after half of time.
Shrimp—1 to 2-lbs. (raw, unpeeled)	2-qt. casserole	Lid or plastic wrap	HI (10)	7 to 10 min.	Stir after half of time.

14　Vegetables

1. Always use microwave-safe utensils, glass or plastic. Cook most vegetables with tight cover to steam them. Exceptions are potatoes cooked in their skins and watery vegetables which need no water added for steam.
2. Do not salt tops of vegetables before microwaving. If desired, add salt to water in dish before adding vegetables. Salt can sometimes cause brown spots on vegetables during microwaving.
3. Cooking time for vegetables affects finished taste and texture. Minimum time on chart gives fresh taste and crisp-tender texture. For soft texture with well developed flavor, cook maximum time or longer.
4. Size of pieces affects cooking time. Large pieces generally take longer than small uniform pieces.
5. Just as when cooking conventionally, vegetable mixtures should have similar densities or degrees of firmness in order to cook together successfully. Firm, crisp vegetables like carrots, cauliflower, broccoli microwave together well. If microwaving a firm vegetable with a soft one (carrots and peas, for example) cut the carrots in julienne strips so they will cook as fast as the peas. Or, start cooking larger carrot pieces first, and add peas during last few minutes.

VEGETABLES	Container	Cover	Power Level	Microwave Time	Comments
Slices, pieces	Casserole	Yes	1-lb.: HI (10) 2-lbs.: HI (10)	11 to 17 min. 15 to 20 min.	Add ¼ to ½ cup water. If frozen reduce time 3 to 5 minutes.
Whole-Halves or large or starchy vegetables (Potatoes, winter squash, cauliflower, etc.)	Potatoes: Cook on oven floor (no container) Other vegetables: square or oblong dish or casserole	No No	1-lb. (3 to 4): HI (10) 2-lbs. (6 to 8): HI (10)	12 to 20 min. 16 to 20 min.	Prick skin of potatoes before cooking. Also see pages 72–75 for more information.
Watery (Tomatoes, Summer Squash)	Casserole	Yes	1-lb. (3 to 4): HI (10) 2-lbs. (6 to 8): HI (10)	4 to 12 min. 6 to 15 min.	Cut in pieces or halves. No additional water needed.
Vegetable Casseroles	Casserole	Yes	Casserole made with raw vegetables: HI (10) Precooked vegetables: HI (10)	15 to 20 min. 10 to 12 min.	Use large enough casserole to allow for boiling in dish.
Stir-Fry Vegetables	Casserole	Yes	HI (10)	12 to 14 min. (6 to 8 servings)	See page 77 in recipe.
Blanching fresh vegetables for freezing	Glass casserole	Yes	HI (10)	3 to 5 min.	Blanch only 1-lb. or 1-qt. prepared vegetables at a time. Place in 1 to 2-qt. casserole with ¼ to ½ cup water. Blanched vegetables will have bright even color and will be slightly softened. Cool drained blanched vegetables immediately by plunging in container of ice water.

Gravies & Sauces

1. No cover is needed, except for thick chunky spaghetti sauce.
2. Because microwaved sauces evaporate less than on the range top, they are thinner than conventionally cooked sauces made with the same amount of thickening. Increase thickening by adding extra teaspoon to 1 tablespoon flour or cornstarch for each cup of liquid.
3. Microwaved sauces do not need to be stirred constantly but most should be whisked vigorously with wire whisk once or twice while microwaving.
4. Vary basic white sauce by adding cheese, egg yolks, cream or dry milk solids. Add flour with mayonnaise or wine.

FOOD	Container	Cover	Power Level	Microwave Time	Comments
Gravies and sauces thickened with flour or cornstarch	Glass measure or bowl	No	1 cup: HI (10)	4 to 5 min.	Microwave fat, flour and salt together to melt and blend. Whisk in liquid and finish. Increase time 1 to 2 minutes per additional cup of sauce.
Thin, liquid sauces (Au jus, Clam, etc.)	Casserole	No	1 cup: HI (10)	2 to 3 min.	Add cornstarch-water mixture to heated ingredients. Stir well and microwave to finish.
Melted butter sauces, clarified butter	Glass measure	No	½ cup: HI (10)	½ to 1 min.	Microwave butter just to melt. For clarified butter, bring to boil then let stand until layers separate. Pour off and use clear top layer.
Thick spaghetti, barbecue or sweet/sour sauces	Casserole, large bowl	Yes (spaghetti)	2 cups: HI (10)	5 to 7 min.	Stir ingredients together then microwave, stirring after half of time. Let stand 5 to 10 minutes to develop flavor.

1. Always use microwave-safe utensil, glass or plastic.
2. For pasta use about half the amount of water needed for conventional boiling; there is less evaporation in a microwave oven. Add regular amount salt and 1 teaspoon oil (optional, to prevent sticking).
3. For rice or minute rice use the same or slightly greater amount water as with conventional boiling. Add regular amount salt.
4. Cover pasta and rice tightly while microwaving. When using plastic wrap, turn back one corner to vent.
5. Stir or rearrange after half of cooking time. Drain pasta immediately after microwaving.
6. Microwaving time is about the same as conventional boiling.

PASTA and RICE	Container	Cover	Power Level	Microwave Time	Comments
Macaroni (7-oz.)	3–4 qt. casserole	Lid or plastic wrap	HI (10)	12 to 14 min.	Add 3 cups hottest tap water. For rotini type, check for doneness after 10 minutes.
Spaghetti (16-oz.)	3-qt. oblong glass baking dish	Plastic wrap	HI (10)	16 to 19 min.	Add 6 cups water.
Egg Noodles (8-oz.)	3-qt. casserole	Lid or plastic wrap	HI (10)	13 to 15 min.	Add 6 cups water. Time is the same for spinach or regular noodles.
Lasagna (8 oz.)	3-qt. oblong glass baking dish	Plastic wrap	HI (10)	16 to 18 min.	Cover with water in dish.
Manicotti (5-oz.)	2-qt. oblong glass baking dish	Plastic wrap	HI (10)	16 to 18 min.	Brush with oil then cover with water.
Rice regular long grain (1 cup)	3-qt. casserole	Lid or plastic wrap	HI (10)	18 to 21 min.	Add 2¼ cups water.
Rice minute (1½ cups)	2-qt. casserole	Lid or plastic wrap	HI (10)	4 to 6 min.	Add 1½ cups water. Let stand covered 5 minutes before serving.

Cereal

1. Always use microwave-safe utensils, glass or plastic. Use large enough container to avoid spillover.
2. Start with hottest tap water to shorten cooking time.
3. Do not cover (prevents spillover).
4. Stir half-way through cooking time.

FOOD	Container	Cover	Power Level	Microwave Time	Comments
Oatmeal, Quick	1-qt. casserole or bowl	No	HI (10)	1 to 2 min. per serving	Mix cereal, salt and hottest tap water before microwaving. Stir before serving. For 6 servings, use 3-qt. casserole.

NOTE: To microwave single-serving packet of instant oatmeal, follow package directions for amount of water and microwave at HI (10) for ½ to 1 minute.

Oatmeal, long cooking	1-qt. casserole or bowl	No	HI (10)	2 to 3 min. for 1 serving	Increase casserole size for more than one serving. Increase time about 2 minutes for each additional serving you are cooking.
Grits, Quick	China or pottery bowl, paper bowl	No	HI (10)	3 to 4 min. for 1 serving	Mix cereal with hottest tap water. Increase casserole size and microwave time by 2 minutes per additional serving.

NOTE: To microwave single-serving packet of instant grits, follow package directions for amount of water and microwave at HI (10) for ½ to 1 minute. Stir before serving.

Cream of Wheat	1½-qt. casserole or bowl	No	HI (10)	2½ to 3 min. for 1 serving	Stir every minute. Increase time 1 minute per additional serving.
Cream of Rice	China or pottery bowl, paper bowl	No	HI (10)	1½ to 2 min. for 1 serving	Increase time about 1 minute per additional serving.

16 Cakes and Desserts

1. Always use microwave-safe utensils, glass or plastic.
2. Before adding batter, grease dishes but do not flour. Or, for easy removal, line dish with wax paper or paper towel.
3. Crust on cakes will be soft. Refrigerate cake if firm exterior is desirable for frosting.
4. Fruit desserts will be fresh looking and tasting.

FOOD	Container	Cover	Power Level	Microwave Time	Comments
CAKES Commercial mix	Round or square dish	No	Med-HI (7)	8-in. round dish: 8 to 10 min. 8-in. square dish: 8 to 10 min	Grease dishes before adding batter. Microwave according to pan size. Rotate dish ¼ turn after half of time. Let stand 5 to 10 minutes before inverting to cool.
	Fluted tube cake pan	No	HI (10)	10 to 12 min.	Rotate cake after half of time. Let stand 5 to 10 minutes before inverting to cool.
Basic butter or chocolate cake	Greased 8-in. round glass baking dish	No	HI (10)	8 to 10 min.	Rotate dish ¼ turn after half of time. Let stand on heat-proof counter or wooden board to cool 15 minutes.
Pineapple upside down cake	8-in. round glass baking dish	No	HI (10)	8 to 11 min.	Do not fill more than ½ full. When done, toothpick stuck in cake comes out clean. Invert cake onto plate, let dish stand over cake a few minutes.
Cupcakes—6	Paper lined cupcaker	No	HI (10)	2 to 2½ min.	When cooking several cupcakes, you may notice some will be done before others. If so, remove cupcakes as they are done and continue cooking the rest a few seconds more.
Bar cookies	8-in. square glass baking dish	No	HI (10)	8-in. square dish: 6 to 8 min. 2-qt. oblong glass baking dish: 9 to 11 min.	Grease dish before adding batter. Rotate dish ½ turn after half of time. Cut when cool.
Baked apples or pears	Microwave safe dish or casserole	Lid or plastic wrap	HI (10)	1 to 3 min. per piece	Pierce fruit or peel to prevent bursting.

Candies

1. Always use microwave-safe utensils, glass or plastic. For easy cleanup, melt chocolate in paper wrappers seam side up, or place chocolate in paper bowl to melt.
2. Candies which are boiled become very hot; be sure to handle cooking containers carefully.

FOOD	Container	Cover	Power Level	Microwave Time	Comments
S'Mores	Paper napkin or paper plate	No	HI (10)	10 to 15 seconds	Cover graham cracker with chocolate and marshmallow. Microwave.
Caramel Apples	1 pint (2 cup) measure	No	HI (10)	3 min.	Unwrap a 14-oz. package of caramels into measuring cup. Add 1 tablespoon water. Microwave and stir smooth before dipping 4 apples into mixture.
Marshmallow Crisp	3-qt. oblong glass baking dish	Yes	HI (10)	1 min. to melt butter 2 min. to melt marshmallows	In 3-qt. casserole melt ¼ cup butter. Add 10-oz. package marshmallows. Cover with wax paper and microwave to melt. Stir in 5 cups crispy rice cereal. Press firmly into buttered 12×8-in. dish.
Chocolate Bark	1½-qt. casserole or bowl	Yes	HI (10)	3 to 4 min.	Place 12-oz. package semi-sweet chocolate chips in container. Microwave to melt. Add 1 cup whole toasted almonds. Spread over wax paper on cookie sheet. Chill until firm.

Many of the techniques used in microwaving are the same ones used in conventional cooking. Most of them either speed cooking or promote even heating.

While the techniques may be familiar, their application may be somewhat different because of the unique way in which microwave energy cooks.

Adapting Conventional Cooking Techniques to Microwaving

Covering. In both conventional and microwave cooking, covers hold in moisture and speed heating. Conventionally, partial covering allows excess steam to escape. Venting plastic wrap or covering with wax paper serves the same purpose when microwaving.

Standing Time. In conventional cooking, foods such as roasts or cakes are allowed to stand to finish cooking or set. Standing time is especially important in microwave cooking. Note that the microwaved cake is not placed on a cooling rack.

Arranging on Oven Shelf. In conventional baking, you position foods, such as tomatoes or potatoes, so that hot air can flow around them. When microwaving, you arrange foods in a ring, so that all sides are exposed to microwave energy.

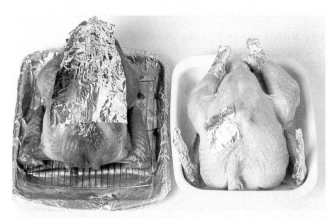

Shielding. In a conventional oven you shield turkey breasts or baked foods to prevent over-browning. When defrosting, you use strips of foil to shield thin parts, such as the tips of wings and legs on poultry, which would cook before larger parts were defrosted.

Stirring. In range-top cooking, you stir foods up from the bottom to help them heat evenly. When microwaving you stir cooked portions from the outside to the center. Foods which require constant stirring conventionally will need only occasional stirring.

Boiling. Microwaves exaggerate boiling in milk-based foods. A temperature probe turns off the oven when the desired temperature is reached. Insert probe so tip of probe is covered by no more than 1 inch of liquid.

Bury Vulnerable Foods. Foods which attract microwave energy, such as cheese or meat, should, when possible, be buried in sauce or other ingredients. In conventional stewing or pot roasting, meat not covered with liquid dries out.

Prick Foods to Release Pressure. Steam builds up pressure in foods which are tightly covered by a skin or membrane. Prick potatoes (as you do conventionally), egg yolks and chicken livers to prevent bursting.

A Technique Unique to Microwaving

Turning Over. In range top cooking you turn over foods such as hamburgers, so both sides can directly contact hot pan. When microwaving, turning is often needed during defrosting, or when cooking foods such as hamburgers from the frozen state.

Rotating. Occasionally, repositioning a dish in the oven helps food cook evenly. To rotate ½ turn, turn the dish until the side which was to the back of the oven is to the front. To rotate ¼ turn, turn the dish until the side which was to the back of the oven is to the side.

Several factors which influence timing and results in conventional cooking are exaggerated by microwave speed. From conventional cooking you are familiar with the idea that more food takes more time. Two cups of water take longer to boil than one. Size and shape of foods are important, too. Cut-up potatoes cook faster than whole ones, and round shapes microwave more evenly than angular ones. The delicacy of food is another factor. Lower temperature and longer cooking time keep these foods from toughening.

Understanding Effects of Food Characteristics When Conventional Cooking or Microwaving

In the pictures below you will notice that differences in food size, shape or density effect microwaving time and cooking results more greatly than in conventional cooking. This is because energy penetrates and turns to heat directly in the food. Knowing what affects speed and evenness of cooking will help you enjoy all the advantages of microwaving.

Piece Size. Small pieces cook faster than large ones. Pieces which are similar in size and shape cook more evenly. With large pieces of food, reduce the power setting for even cooking.

Natural moisture of food affects how it cooks. Very moist foods cook more evenly because microwave energy is attracted to water molecules. Food uneven in moisture should be covered or allowed to stand so heat can disperse evenly.

Density of Food. In both conventional and microwave cooking, dense foods, such as a potato, take longer to cook or heat than light, porous foods, such as a piece of cake, bread or a roll.

Quantity of Food. In both types of cooking, small amounts usually take less time than large ones. This is most apparent in microwave cooking, where time is directly related to the number of servings.

In adapting recipes to your microwave oven, often the cooking energy is expressed in more than one way. This is because the microwave industry has not yet determined exactly how microwave power will be expressed in all recipes. The chart below gives you equivalent cooking power for the several ways you may see this in recipes from other sources.

Understanding Power Levels

POWER LEVEL	APPROXIMATE WATTAGE	PERCENT OF POWER	FRACTION OF POWER	GENERAL USES
HIGH (10)	700	100%	1	Boiling candy, puddings, sauces, vegetables, cooking chicken pieces, fish, hamburgers, baked apples, beverages, bar cookies.
MEDIUM HIGH (7)	490	70%	about ¾	Whole vegetables and chicken, loaf-shaped meatloafs, omelets, bread puddings, muffins, cakes.
MEDIUM (5)	350	50%	about ½	Roasting meats by time or temperature cooking, pot roasting, poached eggs, bread loaves, coffee cakes from refrigerated biscuits, and drying homemade noodles.
LOW/DEFROST (3)	210	30%	about ⅓	Most defrosting. Custards, stewing and braising, delicate sour cream dips.
WARM (2)	140	20%	about ⅕	Proofing bread. Slow gentle reheating.

Understanding Cooking Patterns

Cooking pattern or how evenly a microwave oven cooks is another consideration when adapting recipes from one microwave oven to another. Tips such as the ones below help food cook evenly.

Rotate foods ¼ to ½ turn during cooking time for more even cooking from side to side.

Turning over may be necessary for even defrosting and cooking of meats and poultry.

Stirring food once or twice may be necessary if edges become dry, or boil-over.

Utensils you already have may be suitable for microwaving. Oven glass casseroles, cooking dishes, measuring cups and custard cups are common household utensils. Pottery or china dinnerware which does not have gold or silver trim or are glazed with a metallic sheen can be used.

How to Test Your Dishes at Home for Microwaving

Most glass ceramic oven-to-table ware is labeled "suitable for microwave." If you are uncertain about a dish or container, test by measuring 1 cup of water in a glass cup. Place in oven on or beside dish. Microwave 1 minute at High (10). If water becomes hot, dish is microwave safe. If dish heats, it should not be used for microwaving.

What to Look for When Buying Utensils for Microwaving

Casserole Dishes come in varied sizes and materials including individual serving dishes. They go directly from freezer or refrigerator to microwave. Non-stick finishes or smooth surfaces make cleaning easier.

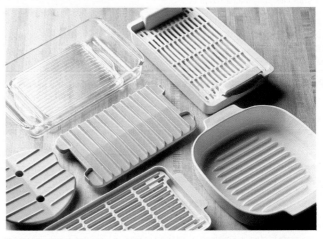

Trivet fits in its own dish or in microwave oven-safe dishes you already have. It holds meat out of juices to prevent stewing. If you don't have a trivet, cook meat on a microwave ovenproof plate or saucer inverted in the baking dish.

Domes are even more convenient than wax paper or plastic wrap when covering foods. They prevent spatters and retain moisture during microwaving. Circular styles cover plates, while rectangular styles are ideal for microwave roasting. Microwave popcorn poppers have dome tops. Domes without venting holes on the top can double as casserole dishes.

Ring Molds (fluted and straight sided) and cupcakers are ideal for cakes, quick bread and meatloaf. All provide the ring shape preferred for microwaving as well as an attractive appearance. Some plastic dishes are available with non-stick coating.

TYPE OF UTENSIL	Microwave Uses
Foil-lined Paper Bags, Boxes and Baking Trays Metal or Part Metal Pots, Pans, Thermometers, Skewers and Foil Trays	Avoid. Use only foil trays ¾-in. or less. Foil or metal will reflect microwaves, thus preventing even heating. Arcing can occur if foil is closer than 1-in. to oven walls.
Boilable Hard and Soft Plastics, such as: Rubbermaid	Cooking ground beef (colander). Defrosting. Heating.
Glass Jars, such as for baby foods, vegetables, entrees, syrups, salad dressing	Do not heat baby food in jars, salad dressings or syrups and other foods in narrow necked bottles.
Handmade Pottery, Porcelain, Stoneware	Cooking and heating.
Microwave Plastics such as: Anchor Hocking Microwave, Bangor Plastics, Mister Microwave, Nordic Ware, Republic, Tara, Wearever Nupac.	Cooking.
Paper or Styrofoam Plates and Cups	Heating and serving foods and beverages. Styrofoam should be used for short-term heating to low temperatures and for serving.
Oven Glass such as: Anchor Hocking, Fire King, Glassbake, Heller, Jena, Pyrex	Cooking and heating.
Regular Dinnerware, such as: Corelle by Corning, Dansk Generation, Denby, El Camino, Franciscan, International Stoneware, Lenox Temperware, Marsh, Mikasa, Pfaltzgraff	Heating and some cooking.
Unsuitable Dinnerware, such as: Corning Centura, Fitz and Floyd Oven-to-table Ware, Melamine, Dishes with metal trim.	None.
Paper Towels and Napkins, Wax Paper	Cooking bacon. Absorbing moisture and preventing spatters. Heating and serving sandwiches or appetizers. Light covering to hold in steam.
Glass-Ceramic (Pyroceram), such as: Corning Ware, Progression G. by Noritake	Cooking and heating.
Plastic Wrap, Cooking Bags, Boil-in-bags, Storage Bags	Covering to hold in steam (wrap). Cooking (cooking and boil-in-bags). Heating (storage bags).
Specialty Glass-Ceramic and Porcelain, such as: El Camino, F.B. Rogers, Heller, Marsh Industries, Pfaltzgraff, Shafford	Recommended for microwave oven-to-table cooking of special foods.

Defrosting

Ice absorbs microwave energy slowly, while water and moisture respond rapidly. Where microwaves penetrate frozen foods and moisture appears, melting is exaggerated. Defrosting techniques which redistribute microwave energy help foods defrost evenly and speed defrosting as well.

Techniques for Even Defrosting

If you try to defrost food without any attention, vulnerable spots, such as edges and thin areas, will start to cook before centers or thick areas are defrosted. Be sure to observe standing time where directed. Some microwave ovens allow you to program standing time.

Flex pouches of fruit, vegetables or convenience foods.

Break up large amounts of hamburger after defrosting.

Thin meaty areas like poultry legs or wings may be shielded during second half of defrost.

Use blunt knife to separate steaks, chops or beef patties.

Use trivet or paper towel to prevent soggy rolls.

Foods which do not freeze well include custard, and some smoked meats.

Many touch control model ovens have a step by step programming feature which allows you to set your microwave oven to Defrost, Hold (no heat), then Time Cook all at one time. The oven will automatically switch power levels for you as cooking progresses. Refer to the use and care book for programming this feature. Because of adding the hold time, this process takes longer but heating is more even.

Tips for Using Step by Step Oven Setting Feature for Frozen Foods

This 3-step cooking process is especially ideal for foods which are uneven in moisture content or composition. Foods with moist or juicy filling and meats with thin bony areas may be defrosted and microwaved this way, as can dense casseroles and meat dishes which tend to cook on the outside edges before the center finishes if not enough holding time is allowed.

Place dry food like pizza, egg rolls, sandwiches and rolls on trivet for dry or crisp texture.

Arrange saucy casserole frosty-side-up in microwave safe casserole to prevent drying.

Warm pie wedges or whole pies. Fruit, nut, pumpkin and custard work well.

FROZEN BAKED GOODS CHART

FOOD	DEFROST TIME (MIN.)	HOLD TIME (MIN.)	COOK TIME IN MINS. (MED. HIGH)
Coffeecake (10 to 20-oz.)	2 to 3	10	2 to 3
Sweet rolls (7 to 10-oz.)	1 to 2	5	1 to 2
Pies			
Whole (20 to 22-oz.)	5	15	3 to 4
Individual (8-oz.)	2	10	1 to 2

How to Cook Many Convenience Foods at Once Using the Oven Shelf

Check empty containers for fit in oven, then add frozen foods.

Arrange entrees and meats on oven floor, vegetables or desserts on top shelf. To determine microwave time, add together times for each food. Check and stir after half of time.

TV Dinners

You can microwave TV dinners at either High (10) or Medium High (7) Power. Medium High results in a more evenly microwaved dinner.

TV Dinner Chart

Size	Cook Time at HIGH (10)	Alternate Cook Time at MED-HIGH (7)
6 to 8-oz. (entree-type or breakfast)	4 to 5	5 to 7
10 to 12-oz. (regular-type)*	6 to 8	9 to 11
16 to 20-oz. (hearty or man-size type)*	9 to 11	11 to 14

*See tip below about avoiding crisp or baked-type foods.

How to Heat Frozen Foods in a Foil Tray

Most TV dinners come in foil trays. These trays can be used in the microwave oven if the precautions stated below are followed. The foil cover must be removed as explained below. Trays should be no more than ¾-in. deep. To avoid electrical sparks (''arcing''), place trays at least 1 inch from oven walls. Foods in deeper trays should be removed to microwave oven-proof containers.

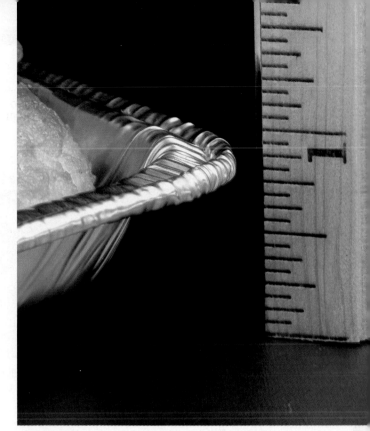

Height of TV foil tray should be ¾-in. or less.

Peel Off foil lid from shallow tray to allow microwaves to enter and heat the food. Return tray to box.

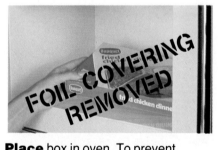

Place box in oven. To prevent arcing, allow at least 1 inch between tray and sides of oven.

Remove box and pull out tray to serve. Stir loose or juicy foods before serving.

Tips for Microwaving Frozen Dinners

Cover dinner plate of food removed from foil tray with wax paper or vented plastic wrap. Follow minimum cooking times on chart, above.

Avoid French fries, batter foods and foods which do not microwave well or remove them from the tray and cook conventionally.

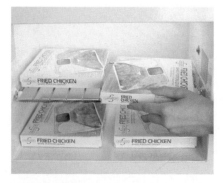

Microwave up to four TV dinners at once by inserting oven shelf. Add together cooking times and reverse positions (top to bottom) of dinners after half of time.

If your microwave oven is equipped with a shelf, use it to double the capacity of your oven. Several ideas for meals using shelf cooking are presented here.

Shelf cooking is a natural when you want to reheat a number of leftovers. Just fit them on the shelf and oven floor, use high power and remove the smallest amounts (which will be done fastest) before the rest.

Tips for Foods and Utensils for Complete Oven Meals

Place empty utensils in oven. Check for fit.

Place main dish, or longest cooking food, on oven floor.

Arrange other foods around main dish or on top shelf.

Techniques for Shelf Cooking

Cover shelf with wax paper or paper towel to prevent top shelf foods from dripping onto foods below.

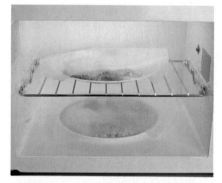

Add total time for all foods, using your cookbook heating guide. Microwave for ½ of time. Reverse (top to bottom) position of plates. Heat for remaining ½ of time. Check foods at minimum time.

Check areas of foods which are close to oven walls. Energy reflected off walls may cook these areas faster than center.

Shelf Cooking

Whether you use the microwave shelf to cook several foods or microwave them one at a time, depends on the type of food and amount of attention you wish to give it. Shelf cooking requires more care than regular microwaving.

Two foods which microwave well at high power may save time when cooked on the floor with a third food on the oven shelf. Microwave timing depends on quantity, two plates of food take twice as long as one; however, both are ready to serve together when you use the shelf.

Techniques for Arranging Foods for Complete Meal Microwaving

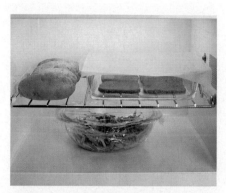

The open arrangement acts like a sieve. Part of the energy is absorbed by foods on both shelf and the floor of the oven, but the spaces between them allow circulation of microwave energy around all foods. With this arrangement it is possible to cook raw foods even on both oven shelves.

The closed arrangement fills an oven shelf closely with food so there is little space for circulation of microwaves. This arrangement requires a little more careful selection of foods because not all the energy is available to each food. Check food after partial cooking and rotate or rearrange if necessary.

The staggered or stacked arrangement allows you to microwave two like foods together at the same time. Small foods have complete access to microwaves by placing one food to the rear of the shelf and one to the front of the oven floor. Larger foods, especially baked items may be stacked with a food on the oven shelf placed directly over the food on the oven floor. Usually food cooked in the stacked position must be reversed after half the cooking time.

Do not use the Brown'N Sear dish on oven shelf. Best cooking results are obtained with this dish on glass ceramic oven floor.

Caution: Oven shelf may be hot, especially after cooking. Large quantities of foods for extended periods. Use oven mitts to remove foods or oven shelf.

28 Appetizers and Hot Snacks

Pictured top to bottom: *Hoagie Sandwich (page 31), Bacon Poles (page 29), Vegetable Platter (page 31) and Stuffed Mushrooms (page 30).*

Soft Smokey Cheese Ball

POWER LEVEL: High (10)
MICROWAVE TIME: 1 to 2 min., total

1 roll-shaped pkg. (6-oz.) smokey cheese spread 2 pkgs. (3-oz. each) cream cheese 1 teaspoon Worcestershire sauce 1 cup (4-oz.) shredded sharp cheddar cheese	Unwrap cheeses. In 1½-qt. casserole place smokey cheese. **Microwave at High (10) 30 Seconds.** Add cream cheese. **Microwave at High (10) 30 Seconds to 1 Minute** more, until cheeses can be mixed together. Add Worcestershire sauce and blend mixture well. Stir in shredded cheese. Mixture should remain gold-flecked.
½ cup chopped fresh parsley ½ cup chopped pecans	Chill cheese mixture about 15 to 30 minutes in freezer or about 1 hour in refrigerator, until it can be formed into a ball with the hands. Roll cheese ball in parsley, then pecans. Chill to set. Serve with crackers.

Makes 1 cheese ball, about 1-lb.

Bacon Poles

POWER LEVEL: High (10)
MICROWAVE TIME: See Recipe

10 strips bacon 20 long, thin garlic bread sticks or sesame bread sticks	With scissors, cut bacon strips in half lengthwise, making 2 long, thin strips from each slice. Wrap one strip in a spiral "barber pole fashion" around each bread stick.

TO MICROWAVE ENTIRE RECIPE: Place 2 paper towels in bottom of 3 qt. oblong glass baking dish. Distribute wrapped bread sticks so they don't touch each other. Cover with paper towel. **Microwave at High (10) 8 to 10 Minutes,** rotating dish ½ turn after 4 minutes, until bacon is cooked. Remove bacon poles as they are done.

TO MICROWAVE 7 ON A PAPER PLATE: Makes 3 plates. Place 2 paper towels on a paper plate. Arrange wrapped bread sticks on top. Cover with paper towel. **Microwave at High (10) 1½ to 2 Minutes,** until bacon is cooked.

Total recipe makes 20

Sugar Glazed Walnuts

POWER LEVEL: High (10)
MICROWAVE TIME: 5 to 7 min., total

½ cup (¼-lb.) butter	In 2-qt. casserole place butter. **Microwave at High (10) 1 Minute,** or until melted.
1 cup brown sugar (packed) 1 teaspoon cinnamon	Stir in brown sugar and cinnamon. **Microwave at High (10) 1 Minute.** Mix well to combine butter and sugar.
1 lb. walnut halves or large pieces (about 4 cups)	Add nuts and mix to coat **Microwave at High (10) 3 to 5 Minutes.** Spread out onto wax paper and cool slightly. Serve warm or cold.

Makes 1 pound

Toasted Butter Pecans

POWER LEVEL: High (10)
MICROWAVE TIME: 4 to 5 min., total

1 lb. pecan halves (about 4 cups) 2 teaspoons seasoned salt ¼ cup butter	In 1½-qt. casserole place pecan halves. Sprinkle with seasoned salt. Cut butter into 4 pieces and arrange evenly over top.

Microwave at High (10) 4 to 5 Minutes. Mix to evenly distribute butter. Serve warm or cold.

Makes 1 pound

Chili Con Queso Dip

Served fondue style, and accompanied by a salad, Chili Con Queso makes a nice informal luncheon. Dip is very thick and should be served with sturdy dippers such as large tortilla chips.

POWER LEVEL: Medium High (7)   TEMP: 140°
MICROWAVE TIME: 6 to 8 min.

1 lb. block pasteurized processed cheese, diced in 1-in. pieces 1 can (1-lb.) chili with beans	In 1½-qt. casserole stir together diced cheese and chili.

Insert temperature probe so tip is in center of dip about 1-in. from top surface. Attach cable end at receptable. **Microwave at Medium High (7). Set Temp, Set 140°.**

When oven signals, stir well. Let stand a few minutes before serving. Serve with tortilla chips.

Makes about 3 cups

Sweet-Tart Franks for a Crowd

POWER LEVEL: High (10)
MICROWAVE TIME: 8 to 11 min., total

In 3-qt. casserole, stir together 2-lbs. frankfurters, cut in 1-in. pieces, and Sweet-Tart Sauce, below. **Microwave at High (10) 6 to 8 Minutes.** Serve immediately or transfer to chafing dish, if desired.

Makes about 80 hors d'oeuvres

Sweet-Tart Sauce

Stir together in small bowl 1 jar (10-oz.) currant jelly and 1 jar (6-oz.) prepared mustard. **Microwave at High (10) 2 to 3 Minutes,** until mixture can be stirred smooth.

Appetizer Franks

POWER LEVEL: High (10)
MICROWAVE TIME: 1 to 2 min., per plate

3 frankfurters **¼ cup apricot preserves or apple jelly** **1 tablespoon prepared mustard**	Cut frankfurters into eighths and arrange in circle on plastic coated paper plate. Mix together preserves and mustard and spread over pieces. Stick each piece with wooden pick. **Microwave at High (10) 1 to 2 Minutes,** until hot.

Chili Franks: Substitute chili sauce for preserves and mustard.

Makes 24 hors d'œuvres

Cheese Pastry Snacks

POWER LEVEL: High (10)
MICROWAVE TIME: 2 to 2½ min., per plate

1 cup (4-oz.) shredded cheddar cheese **¾ cup unsifted all-purpose flour** **¾ cup coarsely crushed crisp rice cereal** **½ cup chopped walnuts** **½ teaspoon garlic salt** **⅓ cup butter, softened** **6 strips crisp cooked bacon, crumbled** **2 tablespoons cold water**	In large mixing bowl mix together cheese, flour, cereal, walnuts, garlic salt, butter, bacon and water with a fork until a dough forms. Drop 7 level tablespoons in a circle onto each of 3 lightly buttered plates suitable for microwave. (Butter plates only around edges, where dough will be placed.)
Paprika	Sprinkle with paprika. Microwave one plate at a time.

Microwave at High (10) 2 to 2½ Minutes, rotating dish ½ turn after 1½ minutes. Dough will be slightly puffed when done and will crisp on drying. Remove immediately from plate. Serve hot or cold. Repeat with remaining mixture.

Makes 21 snacks

Stuffed Mushrooms

Stuffed Mushrooms

POWER LEVEL: See Recipe
MICROWAVE TIME: See Recipe

1. For each of the following stuffings, use 12 to 15 large, fresh mushrooms, 1½ to 2-in. in diameter.
2. Wash mushrooms well, removing stems. Dry.
3. Prepare one of the following stuffing recipes. Divide evenly among caps and mound slightly. Arrange caps in a circle on plate suitable for microwave oven.
4. **Microwave at High (10) 3 to 4 Minutes,** rotating ½ turn after 2 minutes. If mushroom size is not uniform, smaller caps may cook in a shorter time.

Ham or Bacon-Onion Stuffing

Stems from mushrooms, finely chopped **½ cup finely chopped onion**	In 1½-qt. casserole place chopped stems and onion. Cover. **Microwave at High (10) 4 Minutes,** stirring after 2 minutes.
1 pkg. (3-oz.) cream cheese **¼ cup fine dry bread crumbs** **½ cup finely chopped, cooked ham or bacon (8 slices)** **1 tablespoon parsley, chopped**	To hot mixture above, add cream cheese, mashing and mixing well. Stir in crumbs and ham or bacon. Sprinkle with parsley.

Spinach Stuffing

1 pkg. (12-oz.) frozen spinach souffle	Remove from foil container. With sharp knife cut in half. Return half to freezer; place other half in 1-qt. casserole. **Microwave at Medium (5) 1 to 1½ Minutes,** until partially defrosted. Mash with fork.
½ cup soft bread crumbs (1 slice) **1 teaspoon lemon juice** **½ teaspoon instant minced onion** **¼ teaspoon salt**	Mix in crumbs, lemon juice, onion and salt.

Bacon-Wrapped Chicken Livers

This is often known by its Polynesian name of Rumaki. For convenience, you can prepare ahead of time and store in the refrigerator until time to microwave. Because the chicken livers cook more quickly than the bacon, it is important to precook the bacon before using it to wrap the livers.

POWER LEVEL: High (10)
MICROWAVE TIME: 3½ to 5 min., per plate

1 lb. sliced bacon . . . . Divide bacon slices between 4 paper towel lined paper plates. Cover with paper towel. Microwave one plate at a time. **Microwave at High (10) 1 to 1½ Minutes.** Cut each strip in half lengthwise.

1 can (8-oz.) water chestnuts . . . . Drain and cut each chestnut in half.

½ lb. chicken livers (about 20) . . Rinse and drain livers. Cut in half.

Sprinkle bacon strips lightly with ground cloves and brown sugar. Place one piece of chicken liver and one piece of water chestnut at the end of each bacon strip. Roll up, securing with a toothpick. Arrange 10 in a circle on each of 4 paper towel lined (1 sheet) paper plates. Cover with paper towel. **Microwave at High (10) 2½ to 3½ Minutes,** rotating dish ¼ turn after 1½ minutes. When microwaving from refrigerator temperature, increase time for each plate ½ to 1 minute.

Makes 40 hors d'œuvres

Vegetable Platter

POWER LEVEL: High (10)
MICROWAVE TIME: 5 to 7 min., total

2 cups broccoli flowerets
1 cup cauliflower flowerets
¼ cup sliced zucchini
1 sliced carrot
1 medium green pepper, sliced
1 small yellow squash, sliced
¼ cup butter, sliced . . . . . . Select a 12-inch glass platter. Arrange broccoli pieces around outside edge, then cauliflower, carrots and pepper in concentric circles, with squash in the center. Dot with butter slices. Cover with plastic wrap. **Microwave at High (10) 5 to 7 Minutes.**

1 teaspoon seasoned salt
1 teaspoon white pepper . . . . Season with salt and pepper before serving.

Hot Hoagie Sandwich

POWER LEVEL: Medium High (7)   TEMP: 110°
MICROWAVE TIME: 3 to 4 min., total

½ loaf of unsliced Italian or French bread (10 to 12-in. in length)
Mayonnaise
Mustard
½ lb. meat**
3 to 4-oz. sliced cheese*** . . . . Cut bread lengthwise to make two long, thin layers. Spread both cut sides evenly with mayonnaise and mustard, spreading completely to edges. Cover both sides with meat slices, then cover bottom of loaf with cheese.

Place meat covered top half of bread over bottom half. This arrangement results in cheese in center of sandwich with meat on either side. Place on board or platter with piece of paper towel over sandwich and tucked under edges. Insert temperature probe about ⅓ the length of bread loaf so tip is "sandwiched" into center of filling. Attach cable end at receptacle. **Microwave at Medium High (7). Set Temp, Set 110°.** Let stand a few minutes before slicing.

Makes 3 to 4 servings

****Meat Fillings:** Choose thin sliced hard salami, pastrami, pepperoni, corned beef, boiled ham, or a combination of these.

*****Cheese Fillings:** Choose sharp or mild cheddar, brick, Monterey Jack, Swiss, or a combination of these.

Tacos

POWER LEVEL: High (10)
MICROWAVE TIME: 8 to 10 min., total

1 lb. ground chuck beef
½ cup chopped onion
½ cup chopped green pepper
1 clove garlic, minced . . . . In 2-qt. casserole break up ground beef in very small chunks. Add onion, green pepper and garlic. Cover. **Microwave at High (10) 4 to 5 Minutes.** Drain well.

1 can (8-oz.) tomato sauce
1 teaspoon Worcestershire sauce
⅛ to ¼ teaspoon cayenne pepper
½ teaspoon chili powder
½ teaspoon salt . . Add tomato sauce, Worcestershire sauce, pepper, chili powder and salt. Cover. **Microwave at High (10) 4 to 5 Minutes.**

Use meat to fill prebaked, **packaged taco shells,** filling about half full. Finish tacos by topping with 2 or more of the following: shredded lettuce, shredded cheese, chopped tomatoes and chopped onions. Add hot sauce if desired.

Makes 12 tacos

Pictured below, top to bottom Layered Beef Taco Salad (page 37), Teriyaki Spareribs (page 42) and New England Boiled Dinner (page 38).

Ground Beef

Ground beef is a popular part of the American diet. With the microwave oven, it is possible to defrost frozen blocks of hamburger and make fresh hamburger patties in minutes.

You can also microwave other forms of frozen ground beef easily. Frozen blocks go from freezer to cooked crumbled meat in a 1-step process, as can frozen meat balls and loaves. See below.

Defrosting Ground Beef

Packaging affects defrosting time and amount of attention required. Flat, circular packages are easiest to defrost. Tubes should be rotated frequently and broken up as soon as possible. The ends defrost rapidly and may cook before center is defrosted.

Defrost wrapped package on first side according to time in chart below. Turn end-over-end and microwave second side. Packages weighing over 1 pound should be broken up and defrosted meat removed. Defrost remaining frozen parts for additional time.

When defrosted, beef should be cool, soft and glossy. Meat is red and fat is still white (if fat is transparent, meat has begun to cook). Some moisture may be visible. It will make patties that hold together during cooking.

Ground Beef Defrosting Chart   POWER LEVEL: **Defrost (3)**

AMOUNT	FIRST SIDE	Defrosting Time, Minutes SECOND SIDE	BREAK UP & FINISH
1-lb.	4 (Turn package over)	3 to 4	not necessary
2-lbs.	6 (Turn package over)	5 to 6	3 to 4
5-lbs.	12 (Turn package over)	12 to 14 (Remove defrosted meat) 11 to 12	

Freezer to Table Ground Beef

Unwrap 1 pound ground beef and place in cooking container. Microwave at High (10) for 7 to 9 minutes, breaking up and stirring meat after 4 minutes. Some areas may still be pink. Let meat stand 1 to 2 minutes until pink color disappears.

For frozen patties or meat balls, place meat in cooking container called for in recipe. Cover with wax paper. Patties: 4 (¼-lb. each) High (10) 7 to 9 minutes. Meatballs: 12 (1-lb. beef) High (10) 11 to 13 minutes. Both should be turned after half of cooking time.

For meat loaf, use pie-shaped or ring-shaped containers which cook more evenly and quickly than the traditional loaf pan. Microwave at High (10) 27 to 30 minutes, rotating dish ¼ turn after 15 minutes.

Ground beef patties can be served plain or dressed up with a variety of stuffings, seasonings and sauces. Try the suggestions below, then adapt some of your own favorites to microwaving.

Hamburger Patty Stew

When arranging this casserole, be sure that the top layer of beef patties is well covered with vegetables or it will overcook.

POWER LEVEL: Medium High (7)
MICROWAVE TIME: 22 to 25 min., total

2 medium potatoes **2 medium carrots** **2 medium onions**	Peel vegetables and slice into ⅛-in. slices.
1 lb. ground chuck **beef** **1 teaspoon salt** **⅛ teaspoon pepper** **¼ cup water** **Paprika**	Form beef into 12 small flat patties. In 2-qt. casserole layer half of beef patties then half of vegetables, sprinkling layers with salt and pepper. Repeat. Add water. Press down into casserole. Sprinkle with paprika. Cover. **Microwave at Medium High (7) 22 to 25 Minutes.** Let stand 5 minutes before serving.

Makes 4 servings

Bacon Burgers

POWER LEVEL: High (10)
MICROWAVE TIME: 9 to 12 min., total

8 strips bacon	On paper or microwave ovenproof plate place double thickness of paper towel. Layer bacon (4 strips per layer) and separate layers by single paper towel. Cover. **Microwave at High (10) 3 to 4 Minutes,** just until partially cooked.
1 lb. ground chuck **beef** **1 teaspoon salt** **⅛ teaspoon pepper**	Divide ground beef into 8 equal parts; shape into thin patties. Sprinkle patties with salt and pepper.
4 thin slices onion **4 thin slices tomato**	Place one onion and one tomato slice over each of 4 patties; cover with remaining 4 patties and press together edges to seal well.

Wrap 2 partially-cooked bacon slices around to encircle the edges of each hamburger patty. Fasten with toothpicks. Place patties in 8-in. square dish. Cover with wax paper. **Microwave at High (10) 6 to 8 Minutes.** Serve on buttered hamburger buns if desired.

Makes 4 servings

Hamburger (page 10) with Fresh Tomato Garnish (page 76).

Meatballs microwave exceptionally well and turn brown after a short standing time. These recipes are good examples of favorite ways to cook meatballs. However, it is not at all difficult to adapt your own favorite recipes.

Basic Meatballs

POWER LEVEL: High (10)
MICROWAVE TIME: 6 to 8 min., total

1 lb. ground chuck beef **1 egg** **½ cup fine bread crumbs** **1 teaspoon salt** **¼ teaspoon paprika** **⅛ teaspoon pepper**	Mix together beef, egg, crumbs, salt, paprika and pepper. Shape into 12 balls and arrange in a 9 or 10-in. pie plate. Cover with wax paper. **Microwave at High (10) 6 to 8 Minutes** until done. If desired, serve with Italian Sauce, page 66.

Makes 12 meatballs

Arrange meatballs in a ring around the edge of a 9 or 10-in. pie plate. Small meatballs form a double row.

VARIATIONS:
Add one of the following flavor combinations:
1 tablespoon Worcestershire sauce and ¼ cup chopped onion
1 tablespoon steak sauce and 1 clove crushed garlic (or ½ teaspoon garlic powder)
1 tablespoon chili sauce and ¼ cup finely chopped green pepper
2 tablespoons red wine and 1 teaspoon oregano

Swedish Meatballs

POWER LEVEL: High (10)
MICROWAVE TIME: 10 to 14 min., total

2 lbs. ground chuck beef **2 cups soft bread crumbs** **½ cup milk** **1 egg** **1 pkg. (½ of 2¾-oz. box) onion soup mix** **½ teaspoon salt** **½ teaspoon nutmeg**	Mix together beef, crumbs, milk, egg, soup mix, salt and nutmeg. Shape meat mixture into 40 (1-in) balls. Cook 20 at a time in 3-qt. oblong glass baking dish. Cover with wax paper. **Microwave at High (10) 5 to 7 Minutes.** Remove meatballs from dish and keep warm, reserving meat drippings. Repeat.
2 tablespoons unsifted all-purpose flour **1 cup milk** **2 tablespoons browning sauce** **1 cup dairy sour cream (8-oz.)**	To ¼ cup drippings in dish, add flour, stirring until smooth. Gradually stir in milk and browning sauce. **Microwave at High (10) 4 to 5 Minutes,** stirring every minute, until thickened. Add sour cream. Stir well. Return meatballs to dish, mixing to coat evenly. **Microwave at High (10) 1 to 2 Minutes,** until hot. Serve over noodles or rice.

Makes 40 meatballs

Meatballs in Onion Broth

POWER LEVEL: High (10)
MICROWAVE TIME: 40 to 45 min., total

2 pounds very lean ground veal, pork and beef mixture **1 medium onion, finely chopped** **2 eggs** **2 tablespoons flour** **2 tablespoons dry onion soup mix** **1 teaspoon salt** **¼ teaspoon pepper**	In medium bowl mix together ground meat, onion, eggs, flour, soup mix, salt and pepper. Form into medium-sized balls (approximately ¼ cup per ball). Set aside.
Boiling water **2 bay leaves** **2 tablespoons dry onion soup mix** **1 teaspoon salt** **1 teaspoon browning sauce (optional)**	Into 3-qt. casserole pour 4 cups boiling water. Add bay leaves, soup mix, salt and browning sauce. Carefully add meatballs. Add more boiling water if needed to cover. **Microwave at High (10) 40 to 45 Minutes.** Remove meatballs and thicken broth, if desired.

To Thicken Broth: Into hot broth in dish, stir mixture of ¼ cup cornstarch and ¼ cup water. Add additional dry onion soup mix for onion gravy. **Microwave at High (10) 3 to 5 Minutes,** stirring every 2 minutes.

Makes 16 to 18 meatballs

Round flat meat loaves cook fastest at Medium High power (7). Loaf shaped meat loaves need Medium power (5) to evenly cook the center without burning the corners.

Lemon Lovers' Meat Loaf

Lemon juice and lemon slices add tang to this meat loaf.

POWER LEVEL: Medium High (7)
MICROWAVE TIME: 21 to 23 min., total

¾ **cup ketchup**	In small bowl mix together ketchup, brown sugar, dry mustard, allspice and cloves. Set aside.
¼ **cup brown sugar (packed)**	
¾ **teaspoon dry mustard**	
¼ **teaspoon allspice Dash ground cloves**	
1½ **lb. ground chuck beef**	Mix together beef, bread cubes, egg, lemon juice, onion and salt. Mold into rounded flat loaf in 9-in. pie plate.
3 **slices day-old bread, cubed**	
1 **egg, slightly beaten**	
⅓ **cup lemon juice**	
¼ **cup chopped onion**	
2 **teaspoons seasoned salt**	
6 **very thin lemon slices**	Spread half the reserved sauce over loaf and arrange lemon slices on top.

Cover with plastic wrap, turning back one edge to vent. **Microwave at Medium High (7) 21 to 23 minutes.**

When oven signals, remove loaf and let stand 5 minutes to firm. Remove plastic wrap and spread remaining sauce over loaf before serving.

Makes 6 servings

A 1½-lb. Loaf Shaped Meat Loaf can be microwaved at Medium (5) in about 32 to 35 minutes.

Plain meat loaf looks grey. It needs a topping, sauce or browning agent for attractive color. For this picture we brushed the left side of the meat loaf with browning sauce, leaving the right side plain. Because microwave energy is attracted to sweet mixtures, toppings which contain sugar, syrup or preserves can increase over-browning if they come in contact with the bottom edges. When applied before microwaving, they should be brushed only on the top.

When using temperature probe, insert temperature probe as horizontally as possible, so that tip is in the center of the loaf. Cover tightly with plastic wrap, arranging loosely around probe to vent. Microwave to a temperature of 170°.

Basic Meat Loaf

Add ¼ teaspoon herbs or dry mustard to vary flavor. You can make this recipe in a loaf shape by following the tip under the picture at left. Time will be extended but some people prefer the loaf shape in order to make neat slices of leftover meat loaf for sandwiches.

POWER LEVEL: Medium High (7)
MICROWAVE TIME: 21 to 23 min., total

1½ **lbs. ground chuck beef**	Mix together beef, onion, crumbs, egg, ketchup, milk and seasonings. Mold into a rounded, flat loaf in 9-in. pie plate.
¾ **cup chopped onion**	
½ **cup fine dry bread crumbs**	
1 **egg**	
2 **tablespoons ketchup**	
1 **cup milk**	
1 **teaspoon salt**	
¼ **teaspoon pepper**	
⅛ **teaspoon paprika**	
2 **tablespoons ketchup**	Spread ketchup evenly over top of loaf. Cover loosely with plastic wrap. **Microwave at Medium High (7) 21 to 23 minutes.**

When oven signals, remove meat loaf and let stand about 10 minutes to firm before serving. Serve in wedges.

Makes 6 servings

Chili

POWER LEVEL: High (10)
MICROWAVE TIME: 35 to 40 min., total

1½ lbs. ground chuck beef	..Into 3-qt. casserole crumble beef.
1 can (28-oz.) tomatoes, undrained 1 can (6-oz.) tomato paste 2 cans (1-lb.) kidney beans, undrained 1 medium green pepper, finely chopped 1 tablespoon instant minced onion 1 to 2 tablespoons chili powder 2 teaspoons salt	.......Mix in tomatoes, tomato paste, beans, green pepper, onion, chili powder and salt. Cover. **Microwave at High (10) 35 to 40 Minutes,** stirring well after 20 minutes. When oven signals, stir and let chili stand about 10 minutes to blend flavors before serving.

Makes 6 to 8 servings

Cabbage Rolls Italian Style

POWER LEVEL: High (10) and Medium (5)
MICROWAVE TIME: 29 to 33 min., total

8 large cabbage leaves (from outer layers of cabbage) 2 cups water	In 3-qt. casserole place cabbage and water. Cover. **Microwave at High (10) 7 to 9 Minutes,** until leaves are pliable. Drain.
1 lb. ground chuck beef 1 egg 1 cup packaged pre-cooked (minute) rice 3 tablespoons chopped onion 1 teaspoon salt	While cabbage is cooking, mix together ground beef, egg, rice, onion and salt. Divide meat mixture into 8 equal portions. Place one portion on each partially cooked cabbage leaf and roll meat into leaf, securing with toothpick if necessary. Return to 3-qt. casserole, placing rolls seam-side down.
2 cans (8-oz. each) tomato sauce 1 tablespoon sugar 1 teaspoon oregano	Blend tomato sauce, sugar and oregano. Pour over cabbage rolls. Cover casserole.

Microwave at Medium (5) 22 to 24 Minutes, baste with sauce before serving.

Makes 8 cabbage rolls

Layered Beef Taco Salad

POWER LEVEL: High (10)
MICROWAVE TIME: 14 to 17 min., total

1½ lbs. ground chuck beef ½ cup chopped onions 1 cup chopped green pepper 1 can (16-oz.) hot chili beans in chili gravy, undrained	In 1½-qt. casserole crumble beef. Add onion and green pepper. Cover. **Microwave at High (10) for 7 to 8 Minutes,** stirring after 4 minutes. Drain well. Add chili beans. Recover and **Microwave at High (10) for 3 to 4 Minutes,** until hot. Keep warm.
1 can (10-oz.) mild enchilada sauce 1 can (8-oz.) tomato sauce 1 can (8-oz.) mild taco sauce	In 1-qt. glass measure combine sauces. **Microwave at High (10) for 4 to 5 Minutes,** stirring after 2 minutes.
6 to 10 ounce package of corn chips or tortilla chips 1 cup (8-oz.) shredded mozzarella cheese 4 cups shredded lettuce (about ½ head) 2 cups chopped tomatoes	Into 2-qt. salad bowl or casserole layer corn chips, meat mixture, one half of cheese, lettuce and tomatoes. Pour sauce over entire casserole and sprinkle with remaining cheese. Serve immediately, tossing just before serving if desired.

Makes 6 to 8 serving

Sloppy Joes

POWER LEVEL: High (10)
MICROWAVE TIME: 12 to 13 min., total

1½ lbs. ground chuck beef ⅔ cup finely chopped onion ½ cup diced celery ¼ cup diced green pepper	In 1½-qt. casserole crumble beef. Add onion, celery and green pepper. Cover. **Microwave at High (10) 8 Minutes,** stirring after 4 minutes. Drain meat well.
½ cup ketchup 1 tablespoon Worcestershire sauce ½ teaspoon salt ⅛ teaspoon pepper	To cooked meat mixture, add ketchup, Worcestershire sauce, salt and pepper. Cover. **Microwave at High (10) 4 to 5 Minutes,** until hot. To serve, stir, then spoon onto buns or crusty French rolls.

Makes 6 to 8 sandwiches

Sloppy Joes With Cheese: Add 1 cup (4-oz.) shredded cheddar cheese to meat mixture along with ketchup.

Sloppy Joes With Beans: Add 1 can (16-oz.) pork and beans to meat mixture along with ketchup.

Basic Beef Stew

POWER LEVEL: Medium (5)
MICROWAVE TIME: 1 hr. 35 min. to 1 hr. 40 min., total

2 lbs. beef stew meat, cut in 1-in. cubes **1 can (10½-oz.) beef broth** **1½ cups water**	In 3-qt. casserole place beef, broth and water. **Microwave at Medium (5) 60 minutes.**
2 large potatoes, peeled, cut into chunks **5 medium carrots, peeled, sliced** **2 medium onions, sliced** **2 stalks celery, sliced** **½ cup minute tapioca** **1 tablespoon browning sauce** **2 teaspoons salt** **¼ teaspoon pepper** **¼ teaspoon garlic powder**	Add vegetables and other ingredients; combine throughly. **Microwave at Medium (5) 35 to 40 minutes,** stirring 3 times, until meat and vegetables are tender.

Makes about 6 servings

New England Boiled Dinner

POWER LEVEL: High (10) and Low (3)
MICROWAVE TIME: 2 hrs. to 2 hrs. 15 minutes, total

3 to 3½ lbs. corned beef brisket **3 cups water** **1 medium onion, thinly sliced** **2 cloves garlic, minced** **2 bay leaves**	In 3-qt. casserole place brisket with water. Slice onion over brisket and add garlic and bay leaves. Cover. **Microwave at High (10) 20 Minutes.** Turn brisket over. Recover. **Microwave at Low (3) 80 to 90 Minutes,** turning brisket over every 30 minutes. Remove meat from broth and keep warm.
2 large potatoes, cut up **4 medium carrots, cut lengthwise** **1 medium head cabbage, cut in 6 wedges**	Add potatoes and carrots to broth. Arrange cabbage in a pinwheel on top. Cover. **Microwave at High (10) 20 to 25 Minutes,** rearranging after 15 minutes, until vegetables are tender. Discard bay leaves to serve.

Short Ribs and Homemade Noodles

POWER LEVEL: High (10) and Low (3)
MICROWAVE TIME: 1 hr. 37 min. to 1 hr. 45 min., total

2 lbs. short ribs, cut into 2 or 3 rib pieces **1 small onion, sliced** **1 stalk celery with leaves, cut in half** **2 teaspoons salt** **3 cups water**	In 3-qt. casserole place short ribs, onion, celery, salt and water. Cover. **Microwave at High (10) 20 Minutes.** Turn ribs over. Cover. **Microwave at Low (3) 65 to 70 Minutes.**
Homemade Noodles or 1½ cups (½ of 6-oz. pkg.) narrow egg noodles	Remove ribs and keep warm. Add dry noodles to broth. Cover. **Microwave at High (10) 12 to 15 Minutes,** until tender.

Makes 2 to 3 servings

Homemade Noodles

Beat together 1 egg, 2 tablespoons milk and ½ teaspoon salt. Add 1 cup unsifted all-purpose flour and mix to make a stiff dough. Roll out very thin on floured surface; let stand 20 minutes. Roll up loosely; slice ¼-in. wide. Spread loosely in 3-qt. oblong glass baking dish. **Microwave at Low (3) 11 to 13 Minutes,** stirring after 5 minutes, until noodles are dry.

Makes 3 cups cooked noodles

To speed drying spread noodles loosely in glass dish and microwave at Low Power.

Swiss Steak

POWER LEVEL: Medium (5)
MICROWAVE TIME: 50 to 60 min., total

1½ lbs. round steak, ½-in. thick, tenderized or pounded with meat mallet **¼ cup flour** **1½ teaspoons salt** **⅛ teaspoon pepper** **1 medium onion, sliced thin** **1 can (14½-oz.) tomatoes**	Cut meat in 6 pieces, then coat with mixture of flour, salt and pepper. Place in 3-qt. casserole. Cover with onion. Break up tomatoes with fork and pour over top. Cover. **Microwave at Medium (5) 50 to 60 Minutes,** rearranging meat after 30 minutes, until tender.

Makes 6 servings

Swiss Style Cube Steak: Substitute ½-lb. cube steaks, ½-in. thick (about 6), for round steak. Cut in half, if desired.

NOTE: If thicker gravy is desired, stir in 2 tablespoons of flour per cup of juices. Microwave 2 to 3 minutes.

Tender Roast Adapting and Cooking Chart

POWER LEVEL: **Medium (5)**

TYPE		TEMP. SETTING CONTROL	MINUTES PER POUND REFRIG.	COMMENTS
Standing Rib Roast, 4 to 6 lbs.	Rare: Medium: Well:	115° 125° 145°	10 to 12 13 to 15 15 to 17	Place roasts on trivet, fat-side down. Fold any thin ends under boneless roasts, such as tenderloin, and tie with a string. Cover roast loosely with wax paper. Turn roasts over when temperature reaches 90° or after about ½ of time.
Rib Eye and Rolled Rib, 4 to 5 lbs.	Rare: Medium: Well:	115° 125° 145°	10 to 12 13 to 15 15 to 17	
Sirloin Tip, 3 to 4 lbs.	Rare: Medium: Well:	115° 125° 145°	10 to 12 13 to 15 15 to 17	**Allow standing time** of 10 to 15 minutes before carving.
Rolled Rump, 4 to 5 lbs.	Rare: Medium:	115° 125°	10 to 12 13 to 15	Probe not recommended for roasts under 2-lbs. Time cook these roasts.
Tenderloin, whole 4 to 4½ lbs.	Medium:	125°	9 to 11	Turn tenderloin over and rotate dish ½ turn after half of time.
Tenderloin, Half 2 to 3 lbs.	Rare: Medium:	115° 125°	8 to 10 11 to 13	
Pork Loin or Rib, 4 to 5 lbs.	Well:	170°	Cooking Bag: 15 to 17 Wax Paper: 17 to 19	Cooking bag: Place roast fat side up. Make small slit near closure. Wax paper: Place roast fat side down. Add ½ cup water. Cover with wax paper. Turn roast fat side up after ½ of cooking time.
Ham, Precooked: Canned, Butt or Shank	To warm	115°	11 to 13	Place fat side down in dish. (Use trivet for canned ham.) Add ¼ cup water. Cover with plastic wrap, turning back one corner to vent. Turn ham over after ½ of cooking time. Recover and continue microwaving.
LAMB Roast (Leg or shoulder)	Medium: Well:	150° 180°	12 to 14 15 to 17	Place on trivet fat side down. Cover loosely with wax paper. Turn over after ½ of cooking time. Let roast stand 10 minutes before carving. When using temperature probe, insert so tip is not in bone or fat.
VEAL Roast (boneless shoulder)	Medium:	155°	15 to 17	Place on trivet fat or cut side down. Cover loosely with wax paper. Turn over after ½ of cooking time. Let roast stand 10 minutes before carving. Slice thinly.

Less Tender Roast Adapting and Cooking Chart

ITEM	DISH SIZE	POWER LEVEL	TIME, COOK HOURS	AUTOMATIC SIMMER AUTO ROAST CODE 6 HOURS	COMMENTS
Chuck Roast, 3 to 5 lbs.	3-qt. oblong glass baking dish	Medium (5)	1½ to 2	4 to 6	Match cooking container to roast size. Add water, broth or wine. If not adding vegetables, you may use a cooking bag. If cooking dish does not have a vented cover, use plastic wrap, turned back at one corner. Turn meat over after ½ of time.
Sirloin Tip, 3 to 3½ lbs.	3-qt. casserole	Medium (5)	1¼ to 1½	6 to 8	
Beef Brisket, 2½ to 3 lbs.	3-qt. casserole	Low (3)	2 to 2¼	6 to 8	

We recommend using a cooking bag to keep roast pork tender and juicy. Roast fat side up. When using the temperature probe, set for 170°.

Microwaved pork roasts develop browning especially when the fat coating is thin. If the roast has a heavy coating of fat, you may want to brush with a browning agent. Be sure to allow the entire standing time to complete cooking.

How to Defrost Pork Roast

POWER LEVEL: Defrost (3)
MICROWAVE TIME: 8 to 10 min., per pound

If roast is wrapped in paper or plastic, place the unopened package fat side down in microwave safe dish. (Foil wrapping must be removed before defrosting.)
After half of defrosting time turn roast fat side up. Unwrap and shield ends with foil. Rewrap and continue defrosting. Let stand 30 minutes.

Loin end roast. Identified by circular bone at one end of the roast and rack of bones at the bottom. Insert temperature probe into end where the round bone is located, placing it ¾ to 1-in. above the bottom of the roast on the meatiest side of the round bone. Follow bone structure, angling if necessary, so that tip of probe is in the center of the roast. Do not allow tip of probe to touch bone.

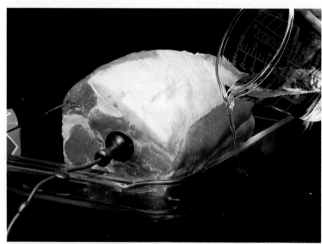

If cooking without a roasting bag, place roast fat side down in dish. Add ½ cup water to roasting dish and cover with wax paper. **Microwave at Medium (5) 15 to 17 Minutes per pound,** turning roast over after half of cooking time. Or use temperature probe set for 170°.

Microwaving Pork Roast by Time

POWER LEVEL: Medium (5)
MICROWAVE TIME: 15 to 17 min., per pound

Place roast in a cooking bag without water. Do not salt roast. Place fat side up in a 3-qt. oblong glass baking dish. Make small slit in bag near closure.

Estimate the minimum total roasting time. **Microwave at Medium (5).** After minimum time, test internal temperature of the roast with a meat thermometer, following instructions given for probe placement. Allow 2 minutes for thermometer to register. If roast has not reached 170°, remove thermometer and return roast to the oven for a few more minutes. When cooking is completed remove and let stand 10 minutes.

Do not place conventional metal meat thermometer in microwave oven.

Cherry Almond Glaze for Pork

POWER LEVEL: High (10)
MICROWAVE TIME: 7 to 10 min., total

1 **teaspoon butter** ¼ **cup slivered almonds**	In 8 or 9-in. pie plate place butter and almonds. **Microwave at High (10) 3 to 4 Minutes,** stirring every 2 minutes, until toasted. Set aside.
1 **jar (12-oz.) cherry preserves** 2 **tablespoons white corn syrup** ¼ **cup red wine vinegar** ¼ **teaspoon salt** ¼ **teaspoon cinnamon** ¼ **teaspoon nutmeg** ¼ **teaspoon cloves**	In 1½-qt. casserole stir together preserves, corn syrup, vinegar, salt, cinnamon, nutmeg and cloves. Cover. **Microwave at High (10) 4 to 6 Minutes,** stirring very well after 3 minutes. Mixture should be well blended. Stir in toasted almonds just before glazing.

Makes about 1¾ cups

Patties containing ground ham do not require use of a browning agent because ham has a naturally attractive pink color; however, a light brushing of browning sauce may be used, if desired.

Sweet 'N' Sour Porkies

POWER LEVEL: Medium High (7)
MICROWAVE TIME: 15 to 17 min., total

1 lb. ground cooked ham ½ lb. ground fresh pork ½ cup soft bread crumbs ½ cup water 1 egg ¼ cup minced celery 2 tablespoons minced green pepper 2 tablespoons instant minced onion ½ teaspoon dry mustard ¼ teaspoon pepper	..In large mixing bowl mix together ham, pork, crumbs, water, egg, celery, green pepper, onion, mustard and pepper. Shape mixture into 4 individual patties and place in 8-in. square dish.
12 whole cloves	Score tops of patties and place 3 whole cloves in top of each.
⅓ cup brown sugar .... 1 tablespoon prepared mustard 1 tablespoon vinegar	Stir together sugar, mustard and vinegar. Pour evenly over patties. Cover dish with wax paper. **Microwave at Medium High (7) 15 to 17 Minutes.**

Makes 4 servings

Classic Ham Loaf

POWER LEVEL: Medium High (7)
MICROWAVE TIME: 19 to 23 min., total

1 lb. ground cooked ham ½ lb. ground fresh pork ½ cup soft bread crumbs ½ cup water 2 tablespoons instant minced onion ¼ teaspoon pepper	..Mix ground ham and pork thoroughly with crumbs, water, onion, and pepper. Mold into flat loaf in 9-in. pie plate. Cover with plastic wrap, turning back one edge to vent. **Microwave at Medium High (7) 19 to 23 Minutes.**

When oven signals, remove loaf from oven, spoon on glaze, and let stand 5 minutes before serving.

Makes 6 servings

Glaze: Stir 4 tablespoons apricot preserves until smooth; spoon and spread on hot ham loaf.

Pineapple Ham and Yams

POWER LEVEL: High (10)
MICROWAVE TIME: 5¼ to 7½ min., total

1 tablespoon butter 1 can (8-oz.) yams or sweet potatoes, drained 2 tablespoons brown sugar 4 slices (about 4-oz.) packaged, thinly sliced cooked ham*	..In 1-qt. casserole place butter. **Microwave at High (10) ¼ to ½ Minute,** to melt. Add drained yams and mash well. Stir in brown sugar. Divide mixture equally over one end of each ham slice. Roll up into firm rolls.
1 can (8-oz.) sliced pineapple	....Drain pineapple, reserving juice. Place pineapple slices in 8-in. square dish. Cover each with ham roll, seam side down.
¼ cup coarsely chopped pecans ¼ cup brown sugar ¼ cup syrup reserved from pineapple	........Combine pecans, sugar and pineapple syrup. Spoon over ham rolls. Cover with wax paper. **Microwave at High (10) 5 to 7 Minutes.**

Makes 4 servings

*Or use thinly sliced leftover ham, about 6-in. long by 3-in. wide.

Fruited Ham Slice

POWER LEVEL: High (10) and Medium High (7)
MICROWAVE TIME: 18 to 22 min., total

1 slice fully cooked ham, 1 to 2-in. thick 1 can (11-oz.) mandarin orange segments 1 can (8¼-oz.) crushed pineapple	....Score or remove fat from ham. Depending on size of slice, place in 8-in. square dish or 2-qt. oblong dish. Drain fruit, reserving juice. Arrange fruit attractively over ham slice. Cover with wax paper. **Microwave at High (10) 10 to 12 Minutes.**
Juice from fruits .... 2 tablespoons brown sugar 1 tablespoon cornstarch ¼ teaspoon ground cloves	Combine juice, sugar, cornstarch and cloves. Pour carefully over ham slice to avoid disturbing the arranged fruit. Cover. **Microwave at Medium High (7) 8 to 10 Minutes,** until hot. Spoon juice over fruit and serve.

Makes 4 to 6 servings

42 Pork Spareribs

The barbecued sparerib is one of America's favorite foods. Few agree on how it should be cooked. Whichever rib you fancy, the microwave oven cooks it fast and flavorful.

Whole Rack of Spareribs should be turned over for even cooking. Rib pieces can be rearranged.

How to Defrost Spareribs

POWER LEVEL: **Defrost (3)**
4 to 7 Minutes Per Pound

1. Place plastic or paper wrapped package in microwave-safe dish. **Microwave at Defrost (3)** ½ of the minimum total time.

2. Turn package over and separate pieces. Defrost for second half of time.

3. Separate remaining pieces and let stand 15 minutes to complete defrosting.

NOTE: For a rack of ribs, turn package over after half of defrosting time. After defrosting, let stand 15 minutes to completely defrost largest end.

Fork Tender Spareribs

POWER LEVEL: Medium (5)
MICROWAVE TIME: 70 to 85 min., total

3 lbs. rack of spareribs **2 cups hot tap water** **1 medium onion, very thinly sliced** **1 lemon, very thinly sliced**	In 3-qt. oblong glass baking dish place spareribs, bone side up. Add water. Cover tightly with vented plastic wrap. **Microwave at Medium (5) 30 Minutes.** Turn ribs over, distribute onion and lemon over top and **Microwave at Medium (5) 30 to 40 Minutes,** until fork tender.
1 cup bottled barbecue sauce	Drain liquid from ribs and pour sauce over top.

Microwave at Medium (5) 10 to 15 Minutes, loosely covered with plastic wrap, until sauce has dried on top.

Makes about 4 servings

TO COOK RIBS IN PIECES: Cut into 2 or 3-rib pieces and microwave in 3-qt. covered casserole.

Teriyaki Spareribs

Ribs may be marinated in sauce several hours or overnight before cooking, if desired.

POWER LEVEL: Medium (5) and High (10)
MICROWAVE TIME: 63 to 74 min., total

3 lbs. spareribs	Have butcher cut rack of spareribs in half crosswise. Cut ribs into 3-in. pieces and place in 3-qt. casserole.
¼ cup soy sauce **1 small onion, thinly sliced** **2 tablespoons brown sugar (packed)** **1 clove garlic, minced** **1 teaspoon ground ginger** **1 teaspoon salt** **1 tablespoon sherry wine** **3 cups apricot nectar or orange juice**	In mixing bowl stir together soy sauce, onion, brown sugar, garlic, ginger, salt, sherry and nectar. Pour over ribs. Cover. **Microwave at Medium (5) 60 to 70 Minutes,** rearranging after 30 minutes. Remove ribs to platter and keep warm. Skim fat from top of liquid remaining in dish.
1½ tablespoons cornstarch **2 tablespoons water**	In small bowl, stir together cornstarch and water. Blend into liquid in dish. **Microwave at High (10) 3 to 4 Minutes,** stirring every minute until sauce is clear and thickened. Serve sauce over ribs.

Makes about 8 appetizer servings, or 4 entree servings

Pork Chops/Steaks

Just as in conventional cooking, texture of pork chops depends upon the cooking method used. Fried chops are chewy; steamed chops are more soft. Some people prefer to brown chops in a skillet on the range top, then finish them by microwaving.

Stuffed 'N' Tender Pork Chops

Because chops are split, each layer of meat is thinner and slightly shorter cooking time may be used.

POWER LEVEL: Medium (5)
MICROWAVE TIME: 25 to 30 min., total

1. Select **4 (1-in. thick) pork chops** with pocket cut in each.

2. Fill pocket with Cornbread Stuffing or Apple Stuffing (below), dividing all of stuffing among chops. Arrange chops in 2-qt. oblong glass baking dish, with thickest meaty areas to edge and "tails" in center. Brush half of glaze over top of chops. Cover with plastic wrap, turning back one corner to vent.

3. **Microwave at Medium (5) 25 to 30 Minutes,** rotating dish ½ turn after 15 minutes, until tender. Let stand 5 minutes. Brush with remaining glaze before serving.

Makes 4 servings

Cornbread Stuffing with Savory Glaze

2 cups crumbled cornbread	In mixing bowl toss together cornbread, onion, green pepper, butter, egg, pimiento, salt and pepper. Divide evenly between chops.
¼ cup chopped onion	
¼ cup chopped green pepper	
¼ cup butter, melted	
1 egg, beaten	
1 tablespoon chopped pimiento	
½ teaspoon salt	
⅛ teaspoon pepper	

Savory Glaze: Mix together ½ cup ketchup, 2 tablespoons brown sugar, 2 teaspoons prepared mustard and ¼ teaspoon chili powder.

Makes about 1 cup

Apple Stuffing with Sweet Glaze

2 cups chopped apples	In mixing bowl combine apples, raisins, egg, butter, cinnamon, salt and pepper. Divide evenly between chops.
¼ cup raisins	
1 egg, beaten	
2 tablespoons butter, melted	
½ teaspoon cinnamon	
½ teaspoon salt	
⅛ teaspoon pepper	

Sweet Glaze: Mix together ⅓ cup currant jelly and 2 tablespoons orange juice.

Makes about ½ cup

Cornbread Stuffed 'N' Tender Pork Chops

Pork Chops Rosado

This dish is very saucy, so plan rice or noodles to serve under chops and sauce.

POWER LEVEL: Medium (5)
MICROWAVE TIME: 30 to 35 min., total

4 center cut loin pork chops, 1-in. thick	In 2-qt. oblong glass baking dish arrange pork chops with thickest meaty areas to edge and "tails" in center. Place onion and lemon slices over top of chops.
1 large onion, cut in ¼-in. slices	
1 medium lemon or lime, cut in ⅛-in. slices	
1 cup ketchup	Combine ketchup and sour cream. Pour over top. Cover dish with plastic wrap, turning back one corner to vent.
1 cup (8-oz.) dairy sour cream	

Microwave at Medium (5) 30 to 35 Minutes, rotating dish ½ turn after 15 minutes, until pork chops are tender. Let stand, covered about 5 minutes before serving.

Makes 4 servings

44 Pork

Fresh raw pork pieces microwave well in saucy casseroles like Sweet and Sour Pork. Just like beef stew meat and other meats requiring tenderizing, they should be cooked until tender at power levels no higher than Medium (5). Casseroles with precooked pork may be reheated at High (10).

Sweet and Sour Pork

POWER LEVEL: Medium (5) and Medium High (7)
MICROWAVE TIME: 32 to 40 min., total

1½ lbs. fresh pork, cut into 1-in. cubes
2 tablespoons instant minced onion
1 tablespoon soy sauce
1 teaspoon browning sauce
1 can (8¾-oz.) pineapple chunks

In 2-qt. casserole place pork, onion, soy sauce and browning sauce. Reserving juice, drain pineapple. Set aside. Add reserved juice to meat, stirring well. Cover. **Microwave at Medium (5) 20 to 25 Minutes,** stirring after 15 minutes.

1 cup water
¼ cup cider vinegar
¼ cup brown sugar
3 tablespoons cornstarch
½ teaspoon salt
1 can (8-oz.) sliced water chestnuts, drained
1 medium green pepper, sliced in ½-in. strips

In small bowl stir together water, vinegar, brown sugar, cornstarch and salt. Add to meat along with pineapple and water chestnuts. Cover. **Microwave at Medium High (7) 12 to 15 Minutes,** stirring and adding green pepper after 8 minutes, until thickened and clear.

1 medium firm tomato, cut into chunks

Fold in tomato chunks and let stand, covered, 10 minutes before serving. Serve over rice or crisp noodles.

Makes 6 servings

Sweet and Sour Pork

Golden Pork Casserole

POWER LEVEL: High (10)
MICROWAVE TIME: 7 to 9 min., total

4 to 6 slices cooked pork roast, ½-in. thick
1 can (17-oz.) yams, drained and cut in 1-in. slices
1 cup coarsely shredded, unpeeled apple
½ cup grated sharp cheddar cheese
3 tablespoons brown sugar
1 tablespoon lemon juice
2 tablespoons butter

In 2-qt. casserole layer pork, yams, apple and cheese. Sprinkle with brown sugar and lemon juice. Dot with butter. Cover. **Microwave at High (10) 7 to 9 Minutes,** until hot throughout.

Makes 4 to 6 servings

Chow Mein

POWER LEVEL: High (10)
MICROWAVE TIME: 22 to 25 min., total

⅓ cup soy sauce
3 tablespoons cornstarch
2 cans (8-oz. each) sliced water chestnuts, undrained
1 can (1-lb.) bean sprouts, undrained
1 can (7-oz.) mushroom stems and pieces, undrained
2 cups diced cooked pork or other meat
2 cups ½-in. diagonal sliced celery
1 medium onion, thinly sliced

In 3-qt. casserole stir together soy sauce and cornstarch. Stir in water chestnuts, bean sprouts and mushrooms, then meat, celery and onion. **Microwave at High (10) 22 to 25 Minutes,** stirring well after 10 minutes, until hot and thickened. Stir thoroughly and serve over cooked rice or chow mein noodles.

Makes 4 to 6 servings

Bacon

Microwaving is a superior way to cook bacon. It is spatter-free and there is less curling and shrinkage than with conventional frying.

When cooked until crisp, bacon will be evenly cooked and flat. Just as in conventional cooking, under-crisp bacon may be randomly cooked, with some spots chewy while others are crisp. The amount of sugar and salt used in curing and thickness of slices will also affect cooking results.

How to Defrost Bacon

POWER LEVEL: **Defrost (3)**
3 to 5 Minutes Per Pound

Place unopened package of bacon in oven. Microwave at Defrost (3) for ½ of time. Turn package over and rotate ¼ turn. Defrost second ½ of time. Let stand 5 minutes or until strips can be separated with a rubber spatula.

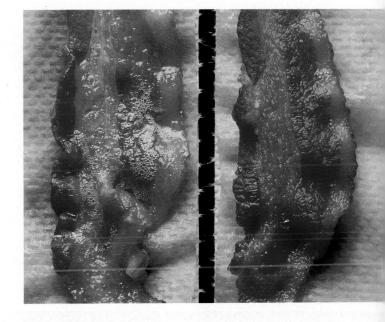

How to Microwave Bacon

The timing below is for average cure, commercially sliced, thin bacon. Cook less time for extra-sweet bacon, more for thick slices.

POWER LEVEL: **High (10)**
¾ to 1 Minute Per Slice

Bacon continues to brown on standing. Left, crisp-cooked bacon as it should look when removed from oven. Right, crisp-cooked bacon after standing 5 minutes.

NOTE: Brown spots on paper towel are due to sugar in the bacon. A high sugar content may also cause bacon to stick to the towel slightly.

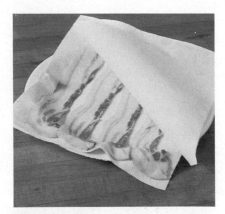

Place two layers of paper towels on paper or pottery plate without metal trim. Arrange bacon on towels and cover with another towel to prevent spatters. Microwave at High (10) ¾ to 1 minute per slice.

Layer bacon when microwaving more than 6 slices. Place 5 slices of bacon on 2 layers of paper towels in a 3-qt. oblong glass baking dish. Cover with a paper towel. Add second layer of bacon. Cover and add more layers as desired. Microwave at High (10) approximately 3 minutes for each layer of bacon. A pound of bacon takes about 12 minutes.

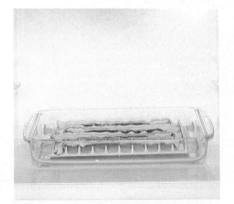

To Save bacon drippings for use in frying, cornbread, or microwave recipes such as wilted lettuce, cabbage or German potato salad, cook bacon on a trivet in a cooking dish. Bacon may also be cooked in a casserole or roasting dish directly in its own fat. As with conventional cooking, remove bacon to paper towel to drain and pour off drippings.

46 Poultry

*Pictured top to bottom: Sweet 'n Tangy Chicken, (page 47),
Microwaved Turkey (page 52), Cornish Hen (page 52).*

Crumb-Coated Chicken

POWER LEVEL: High (10)
MICROWAVE TIME: 13 to 15 min., total

2 eggs . . . . **⅓ cup melted butter** **1 teaspoon salt**	In small bowl beat together eggs, butter and salt.
1½ cups buttery . . . . **flavored cracker** **crumbs (about 50)** **1 chicken, (2½ to** **3½-lbs.) cut up,** **skin removed**	In shallow dish place crumbs. Coat chicken with crumbs, then egg mixture and crumbs again. In 2-qt. oblong glass baking dish arrange chicken with meatiest pieces to outside edges of dish. Cover with wax paper. **Microwave at High (10) 13 to 15 Minutes,** rotating dish ½ turn after 7 minutes.

Makes about 4 servings

Chicken 'n Dressing

For richer flavor, use ¼ cup melted butter for part of chicken broth.

POWER LEVEL: High (10)
MICROWAVE TIME: 22 to 26 min., total

1 pkg. (8 oz.) herb . . . . **seasoned stuffing** **mix** **½ cup chopped celery** **¼ cup minced onion** **2 tablespoons** **chopped pimiento** **1 egg** **2 cups chicken broth**	In 2-qt. oblong glass baking dish toss together stuffing mix, celery, onion, pimiento, egg and broth. Pat down in dish.
1 chicken (2½ to . . . . **3½-lbs.) cut up** **¼ cup butter, melted** **Salt** **Paprika**	Brush chicken pieces with melted butter, place on top of dressing with meaty pieces to the outside edges of dish. Sprinkle with salt and paprika. Cover with wax paper.

Microwave at High (10) 22 to 26 Minutes. Let stand about 5 minutes before serving.

Makes about 4 servings

Spanish Style Chicken

This is a version of the famous Arroz Con Pollo.

POWER LEVEL: Automatic Simmer and High (10)
(Auto Roast Code 6)
MICROWAVE TIME: 4 to 6 hrs.

1 chicken (2½ to . . . . **3½-lbs.) cut up** **1 teaspoon salt** **¼ teaspoon pepper** **¼ teaspoon chili** **powder** **1 clove garlic, minced** **⅛ teaspoon saffron** **powder** **2 cups chicken broth** **2 tablespoons sherry**	In 3-qt. casserole, place chicken with meaty pieces around edges. Sprinkle with salt, pepper, chili powder, garlic and saffron. Add broth and sherry. Insert temperature probe so tip rests in liquid about 1-inch from top surface, halfway between center and side.

Cover tightly with plastic wrap, arranging loosely around probe to vent. Attach cable end at receptacle. **Microwave at Automatic Simmer 4 to 6 Hours.**

To Finish: To casserole, add 2 cups cooked rice, 1 pkg. (10-oz.) defrosted frozen peas and ½ cup sliced stuffed olives. Cover and **Microwave at High (10) 5 Minutes,** until vegetables are hot.

To Microwave by Time Cooking: Assemble chicken, salt, pepper, chili powder, garlic, saffron, broth and sherry in dish and cover according to recipe above. For 1-step setting, set **Time Cook I at High (10) for 17 Minutes, then Time Cook II at Medium High (7) for 18 to 20 Minutes,** cooking chicken until tender. Finish as above.

Makes 4 to 6 servings

Sweet 'n Tangy Chicken

This golden glazed chicken is named for the comments it elicits. It really does taste special.

POWER LEVEL: High (10)
MICROWAVE TIME: 13 to 18 min., total

1 chicken (2½ to . . . . **3½-lbs.) cut up**	In 2-qt. oblong glass baking dish arrange chicken with thickest, meaty pieces to outside edges of dish.
¼ cup mayonnaise . . . . **1 pkg. (½ of 2¾-oz.** **box) dry onion soup** **mix** **½ cup bottled Russian** **dressing** **1 cup (12 oz. jar)** **apricot-pineapple** **preserves**	In small bowl stir together mayonnaise, onion soup mix, dressing and preserves. Spread over chicken, coating each piece. Cover with wax paper.

Microwave at High (10) 13 to 18 Minutes. Allow to stand 5 to 10 minutes before serving, so chicken absorbs flavor of sauce. Serve with rice, if desired.

Makes about 4 servings

Crumb Coated and Spanish Style Chicken (page 47)

Chicken in Italian Sauce
Sometimes known as Chicken Marengo.

POWER LEVEL: Automatic Simmer and High (10)
(Auto Roast Code 6)
MICROWAVE TIME: 4 to 6 hrs.

1 chicken (2½ to 3½-lbs.) cut up 1 pkg. (1½-oz.) spaghetti sauce mix ½ cup water or dry white wine	In 2-qt. casserole, place chicken with meaty pieces around edges. Stir together sauce mix and liquid; pour over top.

Insert temperature probe so tip rests in liquid at center of dish, just below top surface. Cover tightly with plastic wrap, arranging loosely around probe to vent. Attach cable end at receptacle. **Microwave at Automatic Simmer 4 to 6 Hours.** Garnish as described below.

To Garnish: Stir 2 peeled fresh tomatoes, cut in quarters and ¼-lb. fresh mushrooms, cut in ½-in. slices, into chicken. **Microwave at High (10) 3 to 4 Minutes** to heat. If desired, serve with ½ cup sliced black olives and ¼ cup snipped fresh parsley. Serve over rice.

To Microwave by Time Cooking: Assemble chicken, sauce mix and water in dish and cover according to recipe above. **Microwave at High (10) 14 to 16 Minutes,** until chicken is tender. Garnish as above.

Chicken in Wine
Coq au Vin is its French name. This makes a delicious supper when served with rice and a salad.

POWER LEVEL: Automatic Simmer
(Auto Roast Code 6)
MICROWAVE TIME: 4 to 6 hrs.

¾ cup chopped onion 1 chicken (2½ to 3½-lbs.) cut up 1 tablespoon paprika 3 tablespoons minute tapioca Sauce (below)	In 3-qt. casserole, spread onion evenly. Rub paprika on chicken then arrange chicken with meaty pieces around edges. Sprinkle with tapioca. Pour sauce (below) over all. Insert temperature probe so tip rests in liquid just below top surface. Cover tightly with plastic wrap, arranging loosely around the probe to vent. Attach cable end at receptacle. **Microwave at Automatic Simmer 4 to 6 Hours.**
1 lb. large fresh mushrooms, quartered 2 tablespoons fresh snipped parsley	Add mushrooms and parsley to casserole. Cover and **Microwave at High (10) 5 Minutes** to heat.

Makes about 4 servings

Sauce: In small bowl stir together 1 cup white wine, ½ bay leaf, ½ teaspoon thyme, 1 teaspoon salt and ⅛ teaspoon freshly ground pepper.

To Microwave by Time Cooking: Assemble chicken, onion, paprika, tapioca, and sauce in dish and cover according to recipe above. **Microwave at Medium High (7) for 22 to 27 Minutes,** until chicken is tender. Add mushrooms and parsley and finish as in recipe above.

Oriental Chicken

POWER LEVEL: High (10)
MICROWAVE TIME: 8 to 10 min., total

2 chicken breasts split, skinned and boned	Pierce chicken breasts with cooking fork. Arrange in 3-qt. casserole.
1 tablespoon cornstarch 2 tablespoons brown sugar ¼ teaspoon oregano 1 clove garlic, crushed 2 tablespoons cooking oil ¼ cup soy sauce ¾ cup rose wine ⅓ cup seedless raisins	In small bowl combine cornstarch, brown sugar, oregano, garlic, oil, soy sauce, wine and raisins. Pour over chicken. Cover. **Microwave at High (10) 8 to 10 Minutes.** Serve with rice if desired.

Makes 4 servings

Chicken

Mexican Chicken Casserole

POWER LEVEL: High (10)   TEMP: 155°
MICROWAVE TIME: 12 to 14 min., total

1 can (10½-oz.) condensed cream of chicken soup **2 tablespoons green chilies, diced** **¼ teaspoon instant minced onion** **½ cup water**	In small mixing bowl place soup, chilies, onion and water. Stir until well blended.
2 large, firm, ripe tomatoes	Slice tomatoes in ½-in. slices.
1 pkg. (6-oz.) corn chips **2 cups diced, cooked chicken, or 2 cans (5-oz. each) boned chicken, diced** **1 cup (4-oz.) shredded cheddar cheese**	In 2-qt. casserole layer ½ of corn chips. Top with 1 cup chicken, then ½ of tomato slices. Pour ½ of soup mixture over chicken; sprinkle with ¾ of cheese, reserving rest for topping after cooking. Repeat layers.

Insert temperature probe at center of casserole, so tip rests just below top surface. Attach cable end at receptacle. **Microwave at High (10). Set Temp. Set 155°.** When oven signals, sprinkle with reserved cheese and let stand 5 minutes before serving.

Makes 6 to 8 servings

Chicken a la King

The old favorite, creamed chicken, dressed up with colorful pimiento, green pepper and flavorful mushrooms. Serve over toast or in a pastry shell.

POWER LEVEL: High (10) and Medium High (7)
MICROWAVE TIME: 13 to 17 min., total

⅓ cup butter **½ cup unsifted all-purpose flour** **2 cups dairy half & half** **1 cup chicken broth**	In 2-qt. casserole place butter. **Microwave at High (10) 1 Minute,** until melted. Blend in flour. Gradually stir in half & half and broth; mix well. **Microwave at High (10) 7 to 9 Minutes,** stirring with whisk every 2 minutes, until thickened and smooth. Stir well again.
2 cups cubed, cooked chicken **1 jar (4-oz.) sliced pimiento, drained** **1 can (4-oz.) sliced mushrooms, undrained** **½ cup diced green pepper** **1 teaspoon salt** **¼ teaspoon pepper**	Mix in chicken, pimiento, mushrooms, green pepper, salt and pepper. Cover. **Microwave at Medium High (7) 5 to 7 Minutes,** until hot. Let stand 5 to 10 minutes before serving, to blend flavors.

Makes 4 servings

Brunswick Stew

If a more highly seasoned stew is desired add about 1 teaspoon Worcestershire sauce and 3 to 5 drops hot pepper (tabasco) sauce.

POWER LEVEL: High (10)
MICROWAVE TIME: 45 to 53 min., total

1 chicken (2½ to 3½-lbs.) cut up **2 cups water**	In 3-qt. casserole place chicken pieces and water. Cover. **Microwave at High (10) 12 to 14 Minutes,** depending on weight of chicken, until tender. Remove meat from bones discarding skin. Cut meat into pieces and return to broth in casserole.
2 cups diced raw potatoes (2 medium) **½ cup sliced onion (1 small)** **2 teaspoons salt** **¼ teaspoon pepper**	Add potatoes, onion, salt and pepper to casserole. **Microwave at High (10) 15 to 18 Minutes.**
1 can (12-oz.) whole kernel corn, undrained **½ cup unsifted all-purpose flour** **1 pkg. (10-oz.) frozen baby lima beans, defrosted** **1 can (14½ oz.) tomatoes, drained**	Into small bowl drain liquid from corn and stir in flour, mixing well. Blend into hot mixture. Add corn, lima beans and tomatoes. **Microwave at High (10) 8 to 10 Minutes,** stirring after 5 minutes, until vegetables are hot and sauce is thickened. Let stand 5 to 10 minutes before serving, to blend flavors.

Makes about 8 servings

Chicken Almondine

POWER LEVEL: High (10)
MICROWAVE TIME: 6 to 7 min., total

½ cup thinly sliced celery **¼ cup chopped onion**	Combine celery and onion in 1½-qt. casserole. Cover. **Microwave at High (10) 2 Minutes.**
1 can (10¾-oz.) cream of celery soup **¼ cup milk** **½ cup sliced almonds** **1 cup cooked chicken, cubed** **¼ teaspoon Worcestershire sauce**	Add remaining ingredients. Mix well and cover. **Microwave at High (10) 4 to 5 Mintues.** Serve over rice, if desired.

Makes 4 servings

You can dress up whole chicken in a variety of ways, simply by varying the sauce, glaze or topping.

The recipes below illustrate both time and temperature cooking. Depending on the sauce or topping you choose, select the method which gives you the best finished results. Time cooking will produce a drier surface than temperature cooking, which is microwaved in a cooking bag.

Barbecued Stuffed Chicken

We have chosen to cook this recipe by time, instead of by temperature, because of the barbecue sauce coating. The time method uses a loose covering of wax paper which allows steam to escape away from the surface of the bird. As the skin cooks, the barbecue sauce dries to form a beautiful showy glaze.

POWER LEVEL: Medium High (7)
MICROWAVE TIME: 42 to 45 min., total

4 cups day-old ½-in bread cubes or crumbled cornbread **¼ cup minced onion** **½ cup minced celery** **1 teaspoon salt** **1 teaspoon poultry seasoning** **¼ teaspoon pepper** **⅓ cup melted butter** **⅔ cup chicken broth**	In large bowl toss together bread, onion, celery, salt, poultry seasoning, pepper, butter and chicken broth to make stuffing.
1 whole broiler-fryer, about 3-lbs. **Bottled barbecue sauce**	Fill body cavity of chicken with stuffing. Tie wings flat to body with string around chicken; tie legs together. Brush all areas with barbecue sauce.

On trivet in 2-qt. oblong glass baking dish place chicken with breast side down. Cover with wax paper. **Microwave at Medium High (7) 42 to 45 Minutes,** turning chicken breast side up and brushing with barbecue sauce after 15 minutes. Chicken is done when no trace of pink shows in meat when cut is made between inner thigh and breast. Let chicken stand 10 minutes before serving.

Makes 2 to 4 servings

Simmered Chicken

One of the simplest of ways to cook chicken, and one of the best. For ovens with automatic simmer setting included with the Auto Roast feature.

POWER LEVEL: Automatic Simmer (Auto Roast Code 6)
MICROWAVE TIME: Fresh 4 to 6 hrs.
                              Frozen 5 to 7 hrs.

1 whole chicken (2½ to 3½-lb.) Paprika **1 cup chicken broth**	In 3-qt. casserole place chicken. Rub chicken with paprika Add broth.

Insert temperature probe so tip rests in liquid just below top surface. Cover tightly with plastic wrap, arranging loosely around probe to vent. Attach cable end at receptacle. **Microwave at Automatic Simmer 4 to 6 Hours** for fresh chicken, or **5 to 7 Hours** for frozen.

Makes 4 servings

Chicken Teriyaki

Chicken Teriyaki

POWER LEVEL: High (10)   TEMP: 190°
MICROWAVE TIME: 24 to 30 min., total

¼ cup soy sauce **⅓ cup honey** **⅓ cup sherry**	In small cooking bag, mix soy sauce, honey and sherry.
1 whole broiler-fryer, about 3-lbs.	Add chicken to bag and tie open end securely with plastic strip cut from open end of bag.

Turn chicken on its side and place in 2-qt. oblong glass baking dish. Marinate in refrigerator 1 to 2 hours, turning chicken over after ½ of time. To microwave, place bird breast side up in dish. Slash bag near closure. Insert temperature probe through the bag into meatiest part of inner thigh, from below the end of and parallel to the leg. **Microwave at High (10). Set Temp. Set 190°.** When oven signals, remove chicken. Prepare Teriyaki Sauce (below) and finish chicken as described in sauce recipe.

Makes about 4 servings

Teriyaki Sauce: In 1-pt. glass measuring cup stir together 1 tablespoon water and 2 tablespoons cornstarch. Cut off one corner of cooking bag with scissors and drain juices into cup. **Microwave at High (10) 2 to 3 Minutes,** until thick and clear, stirring after 1 minute. After 10 minutes, remove chicken from bag to serving platter. Pour sauce over chicken just before serving.

Since duckling is so fatty, browning sauce is not brushed on before the first half of cooking because it will not adhere to the skin. Add browning agent after partial cooking or broil the bird after microwaving to crisp and brown the thick skin.

Duckling or Cornish Hens Far East Style

POWER LEVEL: High (10)
MICROWAVE TIME: 14 to 16 min., total

2 cornish hens, about 1-lb. each or 1 duckling, about 3-lbs., defrosted	Split in halves, using kitchen shears or a sharp knife. Place in 2-qt. oblong glass baking dish, skin side down.
¼ cup soy sauce **¼ cup sherry wine** **¼ cup pineapple juice** **1 clove garlic, crushed or ⅛ teaspoon garlic powder** **½ teaspoon curry powder** **¼ teaspoon dry mustard**	In small bowl mix together soy sauce, sherry, pineapple juice, garlic, curry powder and mustard. Stir to blend well and pour over meat in dish. Refrigerate 4 to 6 hours, or overnight.

To cook, turn skin side up and baste with marinade. Cover dish with wax paper. **Microwave at High (10) 8 Minutes.** Brush with marinade. Recover. **Microwave at High (10) 6 to 8 Minutes** more, until meat is tender. Serve immediately.

Makes 2 to 4 servings

Duckling with Colorful Marmalade Sauce

Duckling with Colorful Marmalade Sauce

Microwave whole duckling (page 52). During standing time, brush generously with Colorful Marmalade Sauce, below. Let stand uncovered for about 10 minutes before serving.

POWER LEVEL: High (10)
MICROWAVE TIME: 3 to 4 min., total

1 cup sweet orange marmalade **½ cup currant jelly** **1 tablespoon chopped onion** **2 teaspoons soy sauce** **1 teaspoon ground ginger** **½ cup sliced almonds**	In 1½-qt. casserole combine marmalade, jelly, onion, soy sauce, ginger and almonds. **Microwave at High (10) 3 to 4 Minutes,** stirring every 2 minutes, until hot and well combined.

Makes about 2 cups

Brush with diluted browning sauce, if desired. For a crisp skin, omit sauce and, after microwaving, broil under a conventional broiler until crisp and brown.

How to Microwave Turkey In a Cooking Bag

POWER LEVEL: Medium (5) 11 to 13 Minutes Per Pound

Brush turkey with a mixture of 1 tablespoon browning sauce and 4 tablespoons butter. Dry turkey thoroughly before brushing, or sauce will not cling to bird. Shield breastbone area and legs with strips of aluminum foil.

Place turkey in bag and arrange in a roasting dish. If desired, lightly oil inside of bag over breast to prevent sticking. Add ½ cup water, chicken broth, or wine. Close bag securely using plastic tie. Slash bag near closure.

How to Microwave Turkey Without a Cooking Bag

POWER LEVEL: Medium (5) 17 to 20 Minutes Per Pound

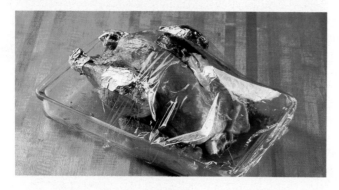

Place turkey, breast side up, on trivet in 3-qt. oblong glass baking dish. Cover with wax paper or plastic wrap. Microwave at Medium (5) for ½ of cooking time. Rotate dish ½ turn. If using temperature probe, insert probe into meatiest area of thigh. Set Temp. Set to 190°. Microwave remaining half of time until probe reaches 190° or legs move freely at joints. Let stand 20 minutes before carving.
Tip: For browner appearance turkey may be brushed with a mixture of 1 tablespoon browning sauce and 4 teaspoons butter before microwaving.

Fruited Rice Stuffing

This recipe may be used to stuff a whole duckling or broiler-fryer chicken (about 3 pounds)

POWER LEVEL: High (10)
MICROWAVE TIME: 6 to 8 min.

In 3-qt. casserole combine 2 cups instant rice, 1 cup golden raisins, 1 cup finely diced celery, 1 small onion, chopped, 1¼ cups orange juice, 1 cup hot tap water, 2 tablespoons butter, 2 tablespoons grated orange peel, ½ teaspoon salt and ¼ teaspoon each pepper, thyme and marjoram. Cover. **Microwave at High (10) for 6 to 8 minutes,** stirring after 4 minutes. Cool.

Makes about 2¾ cups

How to Microwave Cornish Hens and Duckling, Whole

POWER LEVEL: High (10)
MICROWAVE TIME: 4 to 6 Minutes Per Pound

1. Brush hens with browning sauce. (Duckling should not be brushed until second ½ of cooking time.) Shield legs and wings with foil. Place breast side up in 2-qt. oblong glass baking dish. Cover with wax paper.

2. Let stand 10 minutes to allow meat to firm. Test for doneness by piercing thigh with a fork; juices should run clear.

Rice is an excellent stuffing for Cornish Hens and Duckling. For each hen use about ½ cup cooked rice (white and/or wild), well-buttered and seasoned. Use 2 to 2¾ cups of rice for 2 to 3 pound duckling. Or, stuff poultry with Fruited Rice Stuffing (right).

Turkey

Shape as well as size influences defrosting. A broad breasted, meaty turkey takes longer to defrost than a streamlined one of the same weight. Higher areas such as the breast and legs need more shielding because they are higher in the oven.

These directions are for defrosting turkeys weighing up to 12 pounds. If you wish to start defrosting a turkey the day before you plan to roast it, defrost for ¾ time, then place in refrigerator overnight to complete defrosting.

How to Defrost Whole Turkey

Place wrapped turkey, breast side down in oven. It is not necessary to remove the metal closure because of the large amount of food. Microwave at Defrost (3) for ⅓ the time.

POWER LEVEL: Defrost (3) 6 to 7 Minutes Per Pound

Unwrap turkey. Place breast side up on trivet in microwave safe dish. Shield legs, wing tips, and any warm areas with foil. Secure foil with wooden picks it necessary. Continue defrosting. Let soak in cool water or refrigerate overnight to complete defrosting.

Adapting Chart for Whole Turkey and Turkey Parts

Methods: There are two methods below for whole turkey. The method using a cooking bag gives very moist turkey meat and skin. Without the cooking bag, skin is drier and crispier, but cooking time is increased significantly. If your oven has AUTO ROAST, use cooking bag method for whole turkey and Set Auto Roast Code for poultry.

Item	MICROWAVE TIME/MINUTES To Defrost	To Microwave	Power Level	Comments
Whole Turkey 9 to 12 lbs.	6 to 7 per lb.	Without a cooking bag: 17 to 20 per lb.	Medium (5)	Place breast side up on trivet in 3-qt. oblong glass baking dish. Rotate ½ turn after half of cooking time. Let stand 20 minutes before carving. If desired brush with butter and browning sauce. See page 52.
		With a cooking bag*: 11 to 13 per lb.	Medium (5)	See procedure on page 52.
Halves, Quarters and Legs, 4 to 6 lbs.	9 to 11 per lb.	11 to 13 per lb.	Medium (5)	Must be defrosted before microwaving. Brush with butter and browning sauce and cover with wax paper. *Do Not Add Water.* Turn over after ½ of time. Let stand 20 minutes.
Whole Turkey Breast, 6 to 12 lbs.	9 to 11 per lb.	11 to 13 per lb.	Medium (5)	Microwave with temperature probe in cooking bag (see directions for whole turkey, page 52). Insert temperature probe from side into center of thickest meaty area. Set at 170°. Breast cooks to lower finished temperature than whole turkey. Let stand 20 minutes before slicing.

*For complete meal cooking on oven shelf, select turkey no larger than 10 lbs. and use cooking bag technique only.

Hot Turkey and Cheese Sandwich

Hot Turkey and Cheese Sandwiches

These are known in the South as "Hot Browns", created at a famous hotel in Louisville.

POWER LEVEL: Medium High (7)
MICROWAVE TIME: 6½ to 8 min., total

4 strips bacon	On paper plate lined with double thickness paper towels, arrange bacon. Cover with single thickness paper towel. **Microwave at High (10) 1½ to 2 Minutes,** until only partially cooked.
4 slices toast .... **4 to 8 large slices turkey breast** **4 slices tomato (¼-in. thick)** **1 recipe Cheese Sauce, page 66** **¼ cup parmesan cheese**	In 2 (7 to 9-in.) oval au gratin dishes, divide toast, arranging to cover bottoms of dishes. Place 1 to 2 large slices turkey in each dish and top each with 2 tomato slices. Divide cheese sauce over sandwiches. Sprinkle tops of sandwiches with parmesan cheese. Arrange 2 slices partially-cooked bacon over each sandwich.

Place dishes side by side in microwave oven. Cover with wax paper. **Microwave at High (10) 5 to 6 Minutes,** until hot.

Makes 2 sandwiches

Turkey Tetrazzini

POWER LEVEL: High (10)
MICROWAVE TIME: 24 to 29 min., total

1 pkg. (7-oz.) spaghetti	Cook spaghetti (see chart, page 15), except **Microwave at High (10) 9 Minutes.** Drain. Place in greased 2-qt. oblong glass baking dish.
¼ cup butter .... **1 can (4-oz.) sliced mushrooms, drained** **1 small onion, chopped** **1½ teaspoons lemon juice**	In 2-qt. casserole place butter, mushrooms, onion and lemon juice. **Microwave at High (10) 2 to 3 Minutes,** stirring after 2 minutes.
⅓ cup flour .... **1 teaspoon salt** **½ teaspoon paprika** **⅛ teaspoon nutmeg** **2 cups turkey or chicken broth**	Stir in flour, salt, paprika and nutmeg, until smooth. **Microwave at High (10) 1 Minute.** Stir well. Gradually stir in broth. **Microwave at High (10) 6 to 8 Minutes,** until thickened.
½ cup dairy half & half .... **2½ cups cooked, cubed turkey** **½ cup parmesan cheese** **Paprika**	Mix in half & half and turkey. Pour over spaghetti. Sprinkle with cheese and paprika. **Microwave at High (10) 6 to 8 Minutes,** until hot.

Makes 4 to 6 servings

Saucy Turkey and Broccoli

Called Turkey Divan when made with the traditional Mornay Sauce. This makes a nice luncheon or supper dish. A salad of tomato slices is a colorful accompaniment.

POWER LEVEL: High (10)
MICROWAVE TIME: 5 to 6 min., total

1 bunch (about 1¼-lbs.) broccoli, cut in spears	Microwave broccoli according to directions, page 72. Drain. In 2-qt. oblong glass baking dish or microwave ovenproof platter arrange attractively.
8 large slices cooked turkey .... **1 recipe Cheese Sauce, page 66**	Layer turkey slices over broccoli. Cover with sauce. **Microwave at High (10) 5 to 6 Minutes,** until hot.

Makes 4 servings

Pictured top to bottom: Fillets in Lemon Butter (page 57),
Shrimp Gumbo (page 60).

How to Defrost Fillets and Steaks

POWER LEVEL: **Defrost (3)**

ITEM	1st SIDE TIME MINUTES	2nd SIDE TIME MINUTES
Fillets, 1-lb.	4	4 to 6
Steaks, 6-oz.-1	3	1 to 2
Steaks, 6-oz.-2	3	3 to 5

How to Defrost Whole Fish

POWER LEVEL: **Defrost (3)**

ITEM	1st SIDE TIME MINUTES	2nd SIDE TIME MINUTES
1-8 to 10-oz. Fish	3	2 to 4
2-8 to 10-oz. Fish	5	6 to 8
1-3 to 4 lb. Fish	9	12 to 14

How to Defrost Shellfish Frozen in Blocks

POWER LEVEL: **DEFROST (3)**

TYPE	TIME MINUTES
Crab Meat (6-oz. pkg.)	4 to 5
Crab Meat (2 6-oz. pkgs.)	6 to 7
Crab Meat (1-lb. can)	8 to 9
Oysters (12-oz. can)	8 to 10
Scallops (1-lb. pkg.)	6 to 8

How to Defrost Large Shellfish

POWER LEVEL: **Defrost (3)**

TYPE	ROTATE AFTER HALF TIME	TIME MINUTES
Crab Legs (8 to 10-oz.) 1 to 2	yes	6 to 8
Crab Legs (8 to 10-oz.) 3 to 4	yes	10 to 12
Lobster Tails (6 to 9-oz.) 1 to 2	yes	4 to 6
Lobster Tails (6 to 9-oz.) 3 to 4	yes	8 to 10
Lobster Tails (12 to 16-oz.) 1 to 2	no	6 to 8
Whole Lobster or Crab (1½-lbs.)	yes	14 to 16 (approx. 11 min. per pound)

How to Defrost Small Loose Pieces of Shellfish

POWER LEVEL: **Defrost (3)**

TYPE	ROTATE AFTER HALF TIME	TIME MINUTES
Crab Fingers (1-lb.)	yes	7 to 8
Scallops (1-lb.)	yes	6 to 8
Shrimp (1-lb.)	yes	8 to 9

Shellfish Adapting Chart

POWER LEVEL: **High (10)**

TYPE	ROTATE AFTER HALF TIME	TIME MINUTES
Clams (3 to 5-oz.) 6	no	3 to 5
Crab Legs (8 to 10-oz.) 2	yes	6 to 7
(8 to 10-oz.) 4	yes	8 to 10
Lobster Tail (12 to 16-oz.) 1	no	4 to 6
Lobster Tails (8 to 10-oz.) 2	no	5 to 7

TYPE	ROTATE AFTER HALF TIME	TIME MINUTES
Lobster Tails (8 to 10-oz.) 4	no	8 to 10
Whole Lobster (1½ to 2-lb.) 1	yes	9 to 11
Scallops (1-lb.)	yes	6 to 7
Shrimp, peeled (1-lb.)	yes	6
Shrimp, unpeeled (1 to 2-lb.)	yes	7 to 10

Let stand for 5 minutes. Cooking time will be completed during standing time.

Favorite sauces for fish fillets or steaks often include some form of lemon butter as exemplified by two of the recipes here. The third recipe has a creamy sauce, which is another popular accompaniment for fish and seafood.

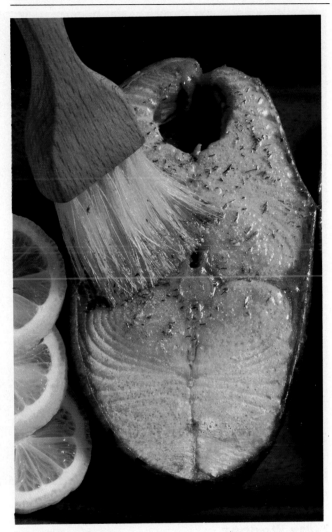

Dilled Salmon Steaks

Fillets in Lemon Butter

POWER LEVEL: High (10)
MICROWAVE TIME: 9 to 12 min., total

1 lb. firm fish fillets . . . . **½ to 1 teaspoon salt** **⅛ teaspoon pepper**	In 2-qt. oblong glass baking dish, arrange fillets with thickest areas to outside edges of dish. Sprinkle with salt and pepper.
½ cup (¼-lb.) butter **½ cup chopped parsley** **1 tablespoon lemon juice** **½ cup buttery flavored cracker crumbs** **½ teaspoon paprika**	In 1-qt. casserole place butter. **Microwave at High (10) 1 to 2 Minutes,** until melted. Blend in parsley and lemon juice and pour over fish. Top with crumbs, then sprinkle on paprika. **Microwave at High (10) 8 to 10 Minutes.**

Makes 4 servings

Dilled Salmon Steaks

POWER LEVEL: High (10)
MICROWAVE TIME: 6 to 8 min., total

4 (½-in. thick) salmon steaks (1-lb.) **2 tablespoons melted butter** **2 teaspoons lemon juice** **½ teaspoon dill weed**	In paper towel lined 2-qt. oblong glass baking dish place steaks. Brush with melted butter mixed with lemon juice. Sprinkle with dill. Cover dish with wax paper.

Microwave at High (10) 6 to 8 Minutes. When done, fish will flake easily with fork. Turn fish over onto serving plate. (Paper towel absorbs juices for best appearance of fish.) Garnish top of steaks with sprinkling of paprika or parsley and additional melted butter, if desired.

Makes 4 servings

Scalloped Fish or Scallops

POWER LEVEL: High (10)
MICROWAVE TIME: 5 to 8 min., total

1 lb. white fish fillets or scallops	On microwave ovenproof platter or 9-in. pie plate place fish fillets or scallops with thickest areas to outside edges of dish. Cover with dampened paper towel which has most of water squeezed out. **Microwave at High (10) 2 to 3 Minutes,** stirring after 1 minute.
¼ cup butter **½ cup soft bread crumbs** **½ cup saltine cracker crumbs**	Remove platter from oven and let stand covered with paper towel while preparing buttered crumbs. In 1-qt. glass measure place butter. **Microwave at High (10) 1 Minute,** or until melted. Add bread and cracker crumbs. Mix with fork.
1 teaspoon salt **⅛ teaspoon freshly ground pepper** **⅓ cup milk or cream**	Remove paper towel from fish and drain. Sprinkle evenly with salt and pepper, then buttered crumbs. Pour milk evenly over top. **Microwave at High (10) 2 to 4 Minutes** more.

Makes 4 servings

Tuna Noodle Casserole

POWER LEVEL: High (10)
MICROWAVE TIME: 14 to 18 min., total

1 pkg. (8-oz.) fine egg noodles	Microwave noodles (see chart, page 15), except cook 8 minutes.
3 tablespoons butter **1 clove garlic, minced** **½ cup finely chopped green onions** **½ teaspoon salt** **⅛ teaspoon pepper**	In 3-qt. casserole place butter, garlic, onion, salt and pepper. **Microwave at High (10) 2 to 3 Minutes,** stirring after 1 minute, until onion is softened.
¼ cup unsifted all-purpose flour **1½ cups milk**	Stir in flour until smooth. Gradually stir in milk. **Microwave at High (10) 4 to 5 Minutes,** stirring every 1 minute, until smooth and thickened.
2 cans (7-oz. each) tuna, drained	Gently stir tuna and drained noodles into sauce. Cover. **Microwave at High (10) 8 to 10 Minutes,** stirring after 5 minutes, until hot.
⅓ cup cracker crumbs **2 tablespoons minced parsley** **2 tablespoons melted butter**	In small bowl, mix together crumbs, parsley and butter. Sprinkle over casserole before serving.

Makes 6 to 8 servings

Scalloped Tuna and Chips

POWER LEVEL: High (10)
MICROWAVE TIME: 11 to 13 min., total

1 can (10½-oz.) condensed cream of celery soup **1 can (7 to 8-oz.) mushrooms, stems and pieces** **1 teaspoon instant minced onion** **1 tablespoon chopped parsley** **1 cup milk** **1 tablespoon lemon juice**	Mix soup, undrained mushrooms, onion, parsley, milk and lemon juice.
3 cups crushed potato chips **2 cans (7-oz. each) tuna, drained and flaked**	In 2-qt. greased casserole layer 1 cup crushed chips, ½ of tuna, ½ of soup mixture. Repeat layers and top with potato chips. **Microwave at High (10) 11 to 13 Minutes,** until bubbly.

Makes 6 servings

Tuna dishes essentially require only reheating by microwave energy because the ingredients are precooked. The three recipes on this page are popular favorites to save you time with family meals.

Tuna Wedges

Tuna Wedges

A tuna loaf, microwaved in a round shape. Garnish with tomato slices and sprinkle with grated cheese if desired.

POWER LEVEL: High (10)
MICROWAVE TIME: 8 to 10 min., total

2 eggs **1½ cups cooked rice** **6 green onions, finely chopped** **2 cans (7-oz. each) solid pack tuna**	In large mixing bowl beat eggs with fork. Add rice, onions and undrained tuna. Mix well.
½ cup (¼-lb.) butter **¼ teaspoon thyme** **1 cup fine dry bread crumbs**	In small glass bowl place butter. **Microwave at High (10) 1 Minute,** until melted. Add to tuna along with thyme and crumbs. Mix well.

Spread mixture evenly in lightly greased 9-in. pie plate. Cover with wax paper. **Microwave at High (10) 7 to 9 Minutes.** Serve in wedges.

Makes about 6 servings

How to Microwave Lobster Tails and Crab Legs

Brush lobster meat with mixture of 1 tablespoon melted butter and 1 tablespoon lemon juice.

Arrange crab legs in baking dish with dark side down. Do not add water.

Cover lobster tails, or crab legs with wax paper and Microwave at High (10), see chart page 56. Turn over after ½ of time. When done, meat is white, not translucent.

How to Microwave Whole Lobster

Plunge the tip of a heavy knife into live lobster between the head and first segment to sever the spinal cord, which kills lobster. Lobster may show signs of movement for a few minutes.

Peg the tail to prevent curling by inserting a wooden skewer lengthwise through the meat. At this time, or after lobster is cooked, cut through the undershell of the body and remove the intestinal vein and small sack below the head.

Arrange lobster in a baking dish with back side down and add ½ cup hot water. Cover tightly with plastic wrap, turning back a corner to vent. **Microwave at High (10) 9 to 11 Minutes.** Turn lobster over after half of time.

How to Microwave Shrimp, Clams and Scallops

ITEM	POWER LEVEL	TIME MIN.	COMMENTS
SHRIMP cleaned, peeled, deveined (1 pound)	HIGH (10)	6	Arrange in ring. Cover tightly with plastic wrap, turning back 2-in. to vent. Rearrange after half of time.
raw, unpeeled (1 to 2 pounds)	HIGH (10)	7 to 10	Place in 2-qt. casserole dish with 2½ cups water, 1 bay leaf, 1 tablespoon vinegar. Rearrange after half of time.

**Shrimp are done when they turn from translucent to opaque.

ITEM	POWER LEVEL	TIME MIN.	COMMENTS
CLAMS 6 (3 to 5 oz.)	HIGH (10)	3 to 5	Place in ring with hinged side out. Remove from oven as soon as shells open partially. Tightly closed shells contain bad clams and should be discarded.
SCALLOPS steamed, 1 pound	HIGH (10)	6 to 7	Arrange in single layer. Cover with damp paper towel. Rearrange after half of time.

Shrimp Gumbo

For spicy flavor, tie 1 to 2 teaspoons crab boil in a cheesecloth bag and add along with shrimp. For bright color accent, save out about ¼ of green pepper to stir into finished gumbo.

POWER LEVEL: High (10) and Medium High (7)
MICROWAVE TIME: 23 to 28 min., total

1 medium onion, sliced (about ½ cup)
¼ cup butter or bacon fat

In 3-qt. casserole place onion and butter. **Microwave at High (10) 3 Minutes,** stirring after 2 minutes, until onion is limp.

2 tablespoons cornstarch
1 cup water
2 cans (14½-oz. each) stewed tomatoes
1 cup diced green pepper (2 medium)
2 cloves garlic, crushed
1 teaspoon salt
½ teaspoon ground nutmeg
¼ teaspoon pepper
1 pound raw shrimp, shelled, deveined
2 pkgs. (10-oz. each) frozen okra, defrosted, cut into 1-in. pieces

In small bowl stir together cornstarch and water. Add to onion along with tomatoes, green pepper, garlic, salt, nutmeg, pepper, shrimp and okra. Stir well. Cover. **Microwave at Medium High (7) 20 to 25 Minutes,** stirring and recovering after ½ of time.

Makes 6 to 8 servings

Scalloped Oysters

POWER LEVEL: High (10)
MICROWAVE TIME: 8 to 10 min., total

3 cans (12-oz. each) frozen oysters, thawed (about 3 cups)

Drain oysters, reserving ¼ cup liquid.

¾ cup butter, melted
2 cups fine soda cracker crumbs (about 40 small squares)
1 teaspoon salt
⅛ teaspoon pepper
⅛ teaspoon nutmeg

In small bowl mix together butter, crumbs, salt, pepper and nutmeg. In 10×6×2-in. dish layer ⅓ of crumb mixture, ½ of drained oysters, then ½ of remaining crumbs, and the rest of the oysters. Top with remaining crumb mixture.

¼ cup milk

Mix milk with oyster liquid and pour evenly over top.

With knife, poke 3 to 4 holes through layers so liquid goes to bottom. **Microwave at High (10) 8 to 10 Minutes,** until oysters are firm when pierced with fork. Sprinkle with ¼ cup parsley.

Makes about 6 servings

Creamed Scallops

The classic dish often known as Coquille St. Jacques. Large scallop shells are natural microwave utensils.

POWER LEVEL: High (10), Med. (5) and Med. High (7)
MICROWAVE TIME: 11 to 14

3 tablespoons butter
1 jar (4-oz.) sliced mushrooms, drained
2 green onions, sliced
¼ cup chopped celery

In 2-qt. casserole place butter, mushrooms, onions and celery. **Microwave at High (10) 2 to 3 Minutes.**

2 tablespoons flour
½ teaspoon salt
¼ teaspoon thyme
1 tablespoon pimiento, chopped
⅓ cup white wine
1 lb. raw scallops

Stir in flour, salt, thyme and pimiento. Add wine and scallops. Stir well. **Microwave at High (10) 4 to 5 Minutes,** until thickened. Stir well.

¼ cup dairy half & half
1 egg yolk, beaten

Stir in half & half and egg yolk. **Microwave at Medium (5) 3 to 4 Minutes.** Stir well.

Divide mixture among 4 scallop shells. Top with Crumb Mixture (below). Cover with wax paper. **Microwave at Medium High (7) 2 Minutes,** until hot.

Makes 4 servings

Crumb Mixture: In small bowl, place 2 tablespoons butter. **Microwave at High (10) ¼ to ½ Minute,** until melted. Stir in ¼ cup fine dry bread crumbs and 2 tablespoons Parmesan cheese.

Sweet and Sour Shrimp

Garnish with chopped bacon and green onion slices.

POWER LEVEL: High (10)
MICROWAVE TIME: 4 to 5 min., total

1 recipe Sweet and Sour Sauce, (page 66)
1 lb. cleaned and cooked shrimp
1 can (8-oz.) pineapple slices, drained

Stir together Sweet and Sour Sauce, shrimp and drained pineapple slices. **Microwave at High (10) 4 to 5 Minutes,** stirring gently after 3 minutes.

Makes 4 to 5 servings

Eggs

*Pictured top to bottom: Eggs Benedict (page 62),
Fluffy Cheese Omelet (page 62).*

Eggs microwave rapidly, and since they are a delicate food, toughen when overcooked. The yolks, which have a higher fat content, cook faster than the whites.

When yolks and whites are mixed together, eggs may be cooked at higher power settings. Omelets, which need time to set, are cooked at Medium (5), while scrambled eggs, which are stirred, are microwaved at High (10). Scrambled eggs are one of many foods which microwave better than they cook conventionally.

Eggs Benedict

POWER LEVEL: High (10)
MICROWAVE TIME: 11 to 14 min., total

4 poached eggs (pg. 13)	Poach eggs and allow to stand as directed.
2 egg yolks **1 tablespoon lemon juice** **½ teaspoon dry mustard** **⅛ teaspoon salt** **½ cup (¼-lb.) butter**	While eggs are standing, make Hollandaise Sauce. In container of electric blender measure egg yolks, lemon juice, mustard and salt. In 1-qt. glass measure place butter. **Microwave at High (10) 1 Minute,** until hot and bubbly. Turn electric blender to highest speed and gradually add butter, blending until creamy and thickened.
8 thin slices (¼-in. thick) Canadian bacon	Just before serving, microwave Canadian bacon which has been arranged in single layer on microwave ovenproof plate. **Microwave at High (10) 2 to 3 Minutes.**
4 English muffins, split and toasted	Assemble Eggs Benedict by arranging 2 slices of Canadian bacon, then a poached egg over each of 4 English muffin halves. Top eggs with Hollandaise Sauce. Butter remaining muffin halves and serve as accompaniment. Garnish with parsley if desired.

Makes 4 servings

Fluffy Cheese Omelet

POWER LEVEL: High (10) and Medium (5)
MICROWAVE TIME: 7½ to 10 min., total

3 eggs, separated **⅓ cup mayonnaise** **2 tablespoons water**	In largest mixer bowl beat egg whites at highest speed of mixer, until soft peaks form. Then in smaller bowl, using same beaters, beat yolks, mayonnaise and water. Gently pour yolk mixture over beaten whites. Fold together carefully.
2 tablespoons butter	In 9-in. pie plate place butter. **Microwave at High (10) 1 Minute,** swirl to coat dish. Carefully pour egg mixture into pie plate. **Microwave at Medium (5) 6 to 8 Minutes.**
½ cup finely shredded cheddar cheese	Sprinkle cheese over omelet.

Microwave at Medium (5) ½ to 1 Minute, until cheese is slightly melted. Quickly run spatula or turner around sides and bottom of dish. Fold half of omelet over the other half. Gently slide onto serving plate. Sprinkle with chives, if desired.

Makes 1 to 2 servings

Jelly Omelet variation: Microwave ¼ to ⅓ cup jelly at **High (10) 1 Minute,** until jelly is soft and can be stirred smooth. Set aside. Follow Fluffy Omelet recipe above **omitting** cheese and mayonnaise. Spoon jelly over half of omelet when set but still glossy on top. Fold plain half of omelet over jelly half. If desired, sprinkle cinnamon-sugar over omelet before serving.

Makes 1 to 2 servings

Egg and Cheese Adapting Chart (Use Microwave safe containers)

ITEM	POWER LEVEL	TIME MIN.	COMMENTS
Scrambled Eggs, 2	High (10)	1½ to 2	Stir after half of time.
Scrambled Egg Substitutes (8-oz.)	High (10)	1½ to 2½	Stir 1 to 2 times till smooth.
Poached Eggs, 2	Medium (5)	1½ to 2	Eggs poach ¾–1 min. per egg. See page 63.
Omelet, 3 eggs	Medium (5)	7 to 10	See recipe idea above.
Quiche (9-in.)	Medium (5)	8 to 18	See page 63.

Quiche is so versatile that wedges make a hearty supper, while small pieces provide a distinctive appetizer.

Microwaved quiche has a tender custard and cooks in about half the time required conventionally.

Golden Onion Quiche

Golden Onion Quiche

POWER LEVEL: High (10) ang Medium (5)
MICROWAVE TIME: 14 to 18 min., total

1 commercially frozen pie crust Worcestershire sauce (about 2 teaspoons)	Remove pastry from foil pan to glass 8-in. pie plate. **Microwave at High (10) 1 Minute,** until softened. With fingers, press firmly in pie plate. Brush inside with Worcestershire sauce. Prick pastry. **Microwave at High (10) 2 to 4 Minutes.**
1 cup (4-oz.) shredded Mozzarella or pizza cheese	Sprinkle cheese over bottom of pie shell.
3 eggs ½ cup whipping cream 3 drops hot pepper sauce (tabasco)	With fork, beat together eggs, cream and hot pepper sauce. Pour over cheese in pie shell.
1 can (3-oz.) French fried onions	With sharp knife, cut through onions in can to chop medium fine. Pour over top and lightly press down.
1 tablespoon dried or frozen chives, or chopped green onion	Sprinkle chives, or onion over top.

Microwave at Medium (5) 11 to 13 Minutes. Let stand about 5 minutes to firm slightly before serving.

Makes 1 (8-in.) pie, about 6 servings

Crustless Vegetable Quiche

POWER LEVEL: Medium High (7)
MICROWAVE TIME: 8 to 10 min., total

1 pkg. (10-oz.) frozen chopped broccoli, thawed and well drained 1 cup (4-oz.) shredded cheddar cheese 1 cup (4-oz.) shredded brick cheese 1 can (4-oz.) sliced mushrooms, well drained ¼ cup chopped onion 3 eggs, beaten ¼ teaspoon salt ⅛ teaspoon pepper ⅛ teaspoon oregano ⅛ teaspoon basil	Drain broccoli very well. In large mixing bowl stir together broccoli, cheeses, mushrooms, onion, eggs, and spices. Pour into well-greased 9" pie plate. **Microwave at Medium High (7) 8 to 10 Minutes.** Let stand about 5 minutes to firm slightly before serving.

Makes 1 (9-in.) pie, about 6 servings

Variation: Frozen chopped spinach, asparagus pieces, or other vegetable may be substituted for the broccoli in Crustless Vegetable Quiche.

Classic Quiche Lorraine

POWER LEVEL: High (10) and Medium (5)
MICROWAVE TIME: 12 to 15 min., total

1 (9-in.) Quiche Pastry (see page 85) 6 strips crisp cooked bacon, crumbled ½ cup grated Swiss cheese 3 green onions, chopped	Reserve 2 tablespoons each of bacon and cheese and 1 tablespoon onion. Sprinkle remaining bacon, cheese and onion over bottom of microwaved pastry crust.
1½ tablespoons flour ¼ teaspoon salt Dash cayenne 2 cups half & half	In 1-qt. measure mix flour, salt, and cayenne. Gradually stir in half & half. **Microwave at High (10) 4 to 5 Minutes,** stirring after 3 minutes.
4 eggs	In 2-qt. casserole, beat eggs. Stir in hot liquid.

Microwave at High (10) for 2 minutes, stirring after 1 minute, until thick. Pour into pastry. Top with bacon, cheese, onion and, if desired paprika. **Microwave at Medium (5) 6 to 8 minutes,** until almost set. Let stand 5 minutes.

Makes 1 (9-in.) quiche

Natural cheese reacts to microwaving much as it does to conventional cooking, but faster. Because of its high fat content it melts quickly and tends to become stringy when overcooked. Where cheese must be cooked for more than a few moments, layer it between other ingredients and use Medium Power (5), or use process cheese, which is less apt to become stringy.

Melted Cheese Sandwich

Lo-Cal Melted Cheese Sandwich
This is lower in calories than grilled sandwiches.

POWER LEVEL: Medium High (7)
MICROWAVE TIME: 30 seconds, total

2 slices bread	In conventional toaster, toast bread.
2 slices processed cheese	Assemble sandwich; wrap in paper towel, **Microwave at Medium High (7) for 30 Seconds.** Makes 1 sandwich.

Cheese Fondue with Natural Cheese
It is important to whisk or stir the fondue every minute.

POWER LEVEL: High (10) and Medium (5)
MICROWAVE TIME: 8 to 9 min., total

1 cup dry white wine **2 tablespoons kirsch (optional)**	In 2-qt. microwave fondue pot place wine and kirsch. **Microwave at High (10) 4 Minutes.**
5 cups (20-oz.) shredded gruyere cheese or Swiss cheese **3 tablespoons flour** **⅛ teaspoon pepper** **Dash nutmeg**	Toss cheeses with flour, pepper and nutmeg, until coated. Stir into hot wine. Cover. **Microwave at Medium (5) 4 to 5 Minutes,** stirring briskly every 2 minutes until melted. Serve with cubes of crusty bread.

Makes about 4 servings

Cheese Enchiladas

POWER LEVEL: High (10)
MICROWAVE TIME: 9½ to 12¾ min., total

1 lb. ricotta cheese **1 egg** **1 cup chopped green onions** **2 tablespoons chopped green chilies** **1 teaspoon cumin** **1 cup (4-oz.) shredded Jack cheese**	In mixing bowl stir together ricotta, egg, onions, chilies, cumin and Jack cheese.
8 fresh corn or flour tortillas, (about 6-in. diameter) or, 10 to 12 canned tortillas (5-in. diameter)	Wrap tortillas in towel. **Microwave at High (10) ½ to ¾ Minute,** until pliable. Divide filling among tortillas. Roll up each one tightly.
1 can (10-oz.) enchilada sauce	In lightly greased 2-qt. oblong glass baking dish place rolls, seam side down. Pour sauce over rolls. **Microwave at High (10) 8 to 10 Minutes.**
2 cups (8-oz.) shredded cheddar cheese	Cover with cheddar cheese. **Microwave at High (10) 1 to 2 Minutes,** until cheese is almost melted.
Sour cream and chopped green onions	Garnish with sour cream and green onions.

Makes 4 generous servings

Cheese Rarebit
Rarebit is a rich cheese sauce served over toast.

POWER LEVEL: High (10) and Medium (5)
MICROWAVE TIME: 7 to 10 min., total

8 oz. pasturized processed cheese, diced **1 tablespoon butter**	In 1-qt. casserole place cheese and butter. **Microwave at High (10) 2 to 3 Minutes,** stirring every minute, until smooth.
¼ teaspoon salt **¼ teaspoon dry mustard** **½ teaspoon Worcestershire sauce** **Dash cayenne pepper** **¼ cup dairy half & half** **1 egg yolk, beaten**	Add salt, mustard, Worcestershire sauce and cayenne pepper. Quickly stir in half & half and egg yolk. **Microwave at Medium (5) 5 to 7 Minutes,** stirring every minute, until hot.

Makes 3 to 4 servings

Gravies and Main Dish Sauces

Pictured top to bottom: Poultry Giblet Gravy (page 66)
Sweet and Sour Sauce (page 66)
Cheese Sauce (White Sauce Variation) (page 66)
Classic Italian Sauce (page 66)

Gravies and sauces microwave easily because there is no scorching or lumping or constant stirring. They save time in cooking and clean-up too.

Make them right in the cup you use for measuring or in the microwave oven proof sauce boat you use for serving.

Poultry Giblet Gravy

POWER LEVEL: Medium (5) and High (10)
MICROWAVE TIME: 19 to 25 min., total

Giblets from a 3-lb. chicken **1 cup water**	In 1-qt. casserole place giblets. Prick with fork. Add water. Cover. **Microwave at Medium (5) 16 to 20 Minutes.** Chop medium fine.
¼ cup poultry drippings **¼ cup flour** **½ teaspoon salt** **¼ teaspoon celery salt** **Dash pepper** **Broth from giblets plus water to make 1¼ cups**	In separate 1-qt. casserole place drippings. Stir in flour, salt, celery salt and pepper until smooth. Stir in broth. **Microwave at High (10) 2 to 3 Minutes,** stirring every minute. Add giblets. **Microwave at High (10) 1 to 2 Minutes** more, stirring every minute, until thickened.

Makes about 2½ cups

Classic Italian Sauce

POWER LEVEL: High (10)
MICROWAVE TIME: 9 to 11 min., total

1 large onion, chopped **3 tablespoons olive or cooking oil** **3 cloves garlic, minced**	In 3-qt. casserole place onion, oil and garlic. **Microwave at High (10) 2 to 3 Minutes.**
2 cans (15-oz. each) tomato sauce **2 cans (6-oz. each) tomato paste** **⅔ cup burgundy, beef broth or tomato juice** **2 tablespoons brown sugar** **2 teaspoons Worcestershire sauce** **1 teaspoon oregano** **1 teaspoon basil** **1 teaspoon salt** **½ teaspoon pepper**	Add tomato sauce, tomato paste, wine, broth or juice, brown sugar, Worcestershire sauce, oregano, basil, salt and pepper. Mix together well. Cover. **Microwave at High (10) 7 to 8 Minutes,** until very hot.

Make about 2 quarts

Sweet and Sour Sauce

This piquant sauce is so versatile that it goes with just about every type of meat, poultry and seafood.

POWER LEVEL: High (10)
MICROWAVE TIME: 5 to 6 min., total

½ cup sugar **2 tablespoons cornstarch** **¼ cup cold water**	In 1½-qt. casserole stir together sugar, cornstarch and water, until well blended.
1 can (8-oz.) crushed pineapple **½ cup chopped green pepper** **1 can (4-oz.) chopped pimiento** **½ clove garlic, mashed** **½ cup cider vinegar** **2 tablespoons soy sauce** **10 drops red hot sauce**	Stir in pineapple, pepper, pimiento, garlic, vinegar, soy sauce and pepper sauce. **Microwave at High (10) 5 to 6 Minutes,** until clear and thickened. Let sauce stand 5 to 10 minutes, to develop flavor, before serving.

Makes about 1¾ cups

Basic White Sauce

POWER LEVEL: High (10)
MICROWAVE TIME: 4 to 5 min., total

2 tablespoons butter **2 tablespoons flour** **½ teaspoon salt**	In 1-qt. glass measure place butter, flour and salt. **Microwave at High (10) 1 Minute**. Stir well.
1 cup milk	Gradually stir in milk. **Microwave at High (10) 3 to 4 Minutes,** stirring every minute until thick and bubbly. For thicker sauce, use 3 tablespoons flour instead of 2 tablespoons.

Makes 1 cup

Cheese Sauce: Add 2 cups (8-oz.) shredded sharp cheese and a dash of cayenne pepper to White Sauce. Stir to melt cheese after microwaving as above.

Mornay Sauce: To White Sauce add 1 cup shredded Swiss, Gruyere or grated Parmesan cheese; 2 teaspoons lemon juice and a dash of cayenne pepper; after microwave as above.

Curry Sauce: Add 1 to 1½ tablespoons curry powder along with flour. Microwave as above.

Pictured top to bottom: Jiffy Spanish Rice (page 68)
Easy Method Lasagna (page 69)
Old Fashioned Oatmeal (page 70)

Cheese Stuffed Manicotti

POWER LEVEL: High (10)
MICROWAVE TIME: 26 to 30 min., total

10 manicotti	Cook manicotti (see chart, page 15), except **Microwave 14 to 16 Minutes.**
1 pkg. (6-oz.) shredded Mozzarella cheese **2 cups (1-pt.) ricotta cheese** **1 cup romano cheese (reserve ½ cup)** **1 can (7¾-oz.) spinach, drained** **½ teaspoon garlic powder** **½ teaspoon salt** **¼ teaspoon pepper**	Combine Mozzarella with ricotta, ½ cup romano, spinach, garlic, salt and pepper. Stuff cooked manicotti with cheese filling. Arrange in 2-qt. oblong glass baking dish.
1 can (15-oz.) tomato sauce **Marjoram**	Pour tomato sauce over top. Sprinkle with remaining romano cheese and marjoram. Cover with wax paper. **Microwave at High (10) 12 to 14 Minutes.**

Makes 4 servings

Noodles Romanoff

A traditional combination of noodles, cheese and sour cream.

POWER LEVEL: High (10)
MICROWAVE TIME: 20 to 22 min., total

1 pkg. (7 to 8-oz.) narrow noodles	Cook noodles (see chart, page 15), except. **Microwave 12 Minutes.** Drain well. Place in 2-qt. casserole.
1 cup cottage cheese **1 cup (8-oz.) dairy sour cream** **½ cup chopped stuffed olives** **1 teaspoon instant minced onion** **½ teaspoon salt** **½ teaspoon Worcestershire sauce** **Dash liquid pepper seasoning (tabasco)**	Add cheese, sour cream, olives, onion, salt, Worcestershire sauce and liquid pepper. Mix well. Cover. **Microwave at High (10) 6 Minutes,** until hot.
1 cup (4-oz.) shredded sharp Cheddar cheese	Sprinkle cheese on top. **Microwave at High (10) 2 to 4 Minutes** more, uncovered.

Makes 6 servings

Jiffy Spanish Rice

POWER LEVEL: High (10)
MICROWAVE TIME: 13 to 17 min., total

1 lb. ground chuck beef **1 cup instant rice** **1 can (1-lb. 12-oz.) tomatoes, undrained, cut up** **1 tablespoon instant minced onion** **1 or 2 tablespoons chili powder** **2 teaspoons salt** **⅛ teaspoon pepper**	In 3-qt. casserole crumble beef. **Microwave at High (10) 5 to 6 Minutes,** stirring after 3 minutes. Drain. Add rice, tomatoes, onion, chili powder, salt and pepper. Cover. **Microwave at High (10) 8 to 11 Minutes.** Stir well. Let stand, covered, about 5 to 10 minutes before serving.

Makes 4 to 6 servings

Creamy Macaroni and Cheese

POWER LEVEL: High (10) and Medium High (7)
MICROWAVE TIME: 16½ to 21 min., total

1 pkg. (7-oz.) elbow macaroni	Cook macaroni (see chart page 15), except. **Microwave 7 to 8 Minutes.** Drain well and return to same casserole.
¼ cup butter	In 1-qt. measure place butter. **Microwave at High (10) ½ to 1 Minute,** to melt.
6 tablespoons flour **1 teaspoon salt** **2 cups milk**	Blend in flour and salt. Stir in milk until smooth. **Microwave at High (10) 4 to 5 Minutes,** stirring with wire whisk after 2 minutes.
2 cups (8-oz.) grated sharp cheddar cheese	Stir in cheese until completely melted.

Stir sauce into drained macaroni, mixing well. **Microwave at Medium High (7) 5 to 7 Minutes,** stirring after 4 minutes. If desired, sprinkle top with paprika or buttered crumbs before serving.

Makes 6 to 8 servings

Quick and Easy Macaroni and Cheese variation:

Omit sauce ingredients from above recipe. To cooked macaroni add 1-lb. pkg. process cheese spread, cut in cubes, and 1 can (5⅓-oz.) evaporated milk. **Microwave at High (10) 4 to 8 Minutes,** until cheese can be stirred in easily.

Makes 6 to 8 servings

Green Rice Casserole

Green Rice Casserole

POWER LEVEL: High (10)
MICROWAVE TIME: 17 to 21 min., total

1 pkg. frozen .... **(10-oz.) chopped** **spinach** **3 eggs** **1 can (12-oz.)** **evaporated milk** **⅔ cup packaged** **pre-cooked** **(minute) rice** **1 pkg. (8-oz.)** **Pasturized** **process cheese** **spread cut in cubes** **½ teaspoon salt** **¼ teaspoon pepper**	Microwave spinach in a 1-qt. casserole at **High** **(10) 5 to 6 Minutes**. Drain well and set aside. Mix eggs, milk, rice, cheese, salt and pepper in 2-qt. casserole. **Microwave at High** **(10) 4 to 5 Minutes**, until cheese melts. Stir well.
¼ cup chopped onion	Add onion and spinach to rice mixture and pour into a 10×6×2-in. baking dish. **Microwave at High** **(10) 8 to 10 Minutes** until center is set.

Makes 6 to 8 servings

Easy Method Lasagna

This spicy version does not require pre-cooking noodles. Noodles will have a firm al dente texture.

POWER LEVEL: High (10) and Medium (5)
MICROWAVE TIME: 43 to 46 min., total

½ lb. ground chuck .... **½ lb. ground pork**	Place meat in colander, set over a casserole bowl. **Microwave at High** **(10) 5 to 6 Minutes.** Break up drained, cooked meat with fork; discard fat.
1 can (6-oz.) .... **tomato juice** **1 can (8-oz.)** **tomato sauce** **1 can (6-oz.)** **tomato paste** **1 medium onion,** **chopped** **1 tablespoon oregano** **2 teaspoons basil** **1 teaspoon salt** **½ teaspoon pepper** **2 garlic cloves,** **minced** **2 teaspoons brown** **sugar** **1 tablespoon** **Worcestershire** **Sauce**	In large bowl mix together tomato juice, tomato sauce, tomato paste, onion, oregano, basil, salt, pepper, garlic, brown sugar and Worcestershire sauce. Stir in drained meat. Spread ⅓ meat sauce over bottom of 2-qt. oblong glass baking dish.
6 lasagna noodles .... **2 cups (1-pt.) ricotta** **cheese** **1 pkg. (8-oz.)** **shredded** **mozzarella cheese**	Place ½ the uncooked noodles over sauce and top with ½ the ricotta cheese; then half of mozzarella cheese and half of remaining sauce. Repeat layers and cover with remaining sauce. Cover with wax paper. **Microwave at** **Medium (5) for 33 to** **35 Minutes.**
½ cup grated .... **Parmesan cheese**	Remove wax paper. Sprinkle with Parmesan cheese. **Microwave at** **Medium (5) for** **5 Minutes.** Let lasagna stand 5 minutes before slicing.

Quick and Easy Lasagna Variation:

Microwave and drain ground chuck and pork as directed above. Mix meat with 2 (15½-oz.) jars of commercial spaghetti sauce. Layer meat sauce with noodles and cheese (use amounts and types called for in above recipe) and Microwave as directed above.

Makes 6 to 8 servings

Cereals microwave in a simple, 1-step process. You don't have to boil the water first, or stir frequently during cooking. Microwaved cereals are easy to clean up since the cereal does not stick to the cooking dish. Family members can microwave single servings of instant cereal in paper bowls. There'll be no dirty dishes in the sink after breakfast.

How to Adapt Cereals

Mix cereal and **hottest** tap water in a bowl large enough to prevent boil-over. Microwave at High (10), uncovered.

Stir well before serving. For softer cereal, let stand a few minutes after microwaving.

Cereal Adapting Chart

POWER LEVEL: **High (10)**

TYPE CEREAL	NO. OF SERVINGS	INGREDIENTS				TIME MIN.
		WATER	SALT	CEREAL	CONTAINER	
Oatmeal, Quick*	1	¾ cup	⅛ teaspoon	⅓ cup	1-qt. casserole	1 to 2
	2	1½ cups	¼ teaspoon	⅔ cup	1½-qt. casserole	2 to 3
	4	3 cups	½ teaspoon	1⅓ cups	2-qt. casserole	4 to 5
	6	4 cups	¾ teaspoon	2 cups	3-qt. casserole	6 to 7
Oatmeal, Old-fashioned	1	¾ cup	⅛ teaspoon	⅓ cup	1-qt. casserole	2 to 3
	2	1½ cups	¼ teaspoon	⅔ cup	2-qt. casserole	6 to 7
	4	3 cups	½ teaspoon	1⅓ cups	3-qt. casserole	6 to 8
	6	4 cups	¾ teaspoon	2 cups	3-qt. casserole	10 to 11
Cornmeal	1	⅔ cup	⅛ teaspoon	3 tbsp.	1-qt. casserole	1 to 1½
	2	1⅓ cups	¼ teaspoon	⅓ cup	1½-qt. casserole	2½ to 3
	4	2⅔ cups	½ teaspoon	⅔ cup	2-qt. casserole	2½ to 3½
	6	4 cups	¾ teaspoon	1 cup	2-qt. casserole	4½ to 5
Grits, Quick*	1	¾ cup	Dash	3 tbsp.	1-qt. casserole	3 to 4
	2	1⅓ cups	¼ teaspoon	⅓ cup	1½-qt. casserole	6 to 7
	4	2⅔ cups	½ teaspoon	⅔ cup	2-qt. casserole	8 to 9
	6	4 cups	¾ teaspoon	1 cup	2-qt. casserole	10 to 11
Cream of Wheat	1	1 cup	⅛ teaspoon	2½ tbsp.	1-qt. casserole	2½ to 3
	2	1¾ cups	¼ teaspoon	⅓ cup	2-qt. casserole	3 to 4
	4	3½ cups	½ teaspoon	⅔ cup	3-qt. casserole	5 to 6
	6	5 cups	¾ teaspoon	1 cup	3-qt. casserole	7 to 8
Cream of Rice	1	¾ cup	Dash	3 tbsp.	1-qt. casserole	1½ to 2
	2	1⅓ cups	¼ teaspoon	⅓ cup	1½-qt. casserole	2 to 3
	4	2⅔ cups	½ teaspoon	⅔ cup	2-qt. casserole	3½ to 4½
	6	4 cups	¾ teaspoon	1 cup	2-qt. casserole	6 to 7

*Single servings of instant oatmeal or grits (about 1-oz. pkg.): Follow package directions for amount of water. **Microwave at High (10) ½ to 1 Minute.**

Vegetables

71

Pictured top to bottom: Twice Baked Potatoes (page 76)
Corn on Cob (page 74)
Yellow Squash and Zucchini Combination (page 75)

Vegetable Microwaving Chart

Salt vegetables after cooking, or put salt in the casserole with the water before adding vegetables. Salting the tops of vegetables before microwaving causes darkening and dried out spots.

VEGETABLE	AMOUNT	PROCEDURE	POWER LEVEL	TIME MINUTES	COMMENTS
Artichokes Fresh	4 medium	Prepare by discarding tough outer leaves. Snip tips with scissors and cut off stems. Place artichokes in 3-qt. casserole. Add 1 cup water. Cover. Rotate dish ½ turn after 7 minutes. Test for doneness: At minimum time, try to pull a leaf from whole artichoke. If it comes away freely, artichoke is done.	High (10)	11 to 13	Drain artichokes upside down before serving. Curry mayonnaise is an easy accompaniment; mix 1 cup mayonnaise with 1 to 2 teaspoons curry powder. Artichokes are eaten by pulling off leaves and, with teeth, scraping tender green inner leaf. Cut heart into chunks and eat.
Asparagus Fresh Cuts	1 lb. (3 cups, cut into 1 to 2-in. pieces)	Place asparagus in 2-qt. casserole. Add ¼ cup water. Cover. Stir asparagus every 3 minutes.	High (10)	8 to 10	
Asparagus Fresh Spears	1-lb.	Place asparagus in 10×6×2-in. dish. Add ¼ cup water. Arrange thicker pieces to outside of dish with tender tops to center. Cover dish with plastic wrap turning back corner to vent.	High (10)	8 to 10	Larger, more mature stem ends should be peeled.
Asparagus Frozen Spears	10-oz. pkg.	Place asparagus in 1-qt. casserole. Cover. Rearrange after 4 minutes.	High (10)	8 to 10	No water is needed with this frozen vegetable.
Beans Dry	1 lb.	In 3-qt. casserole place beans, 4 cups water, ham hock, 1 cup coarsely chopped celery, 1 small sliced onion, 2 teaspoons salt, and ¼ teaspoon pepper. Cover.	High (10) Medium (5)	1 hour and 30 min.	Microwave at High (10) for 30 minutes until boiling, then at Medium (5) until tender. Stir every 30 minutes. May add more water during cooking.
Beans Fresh Green & Wax	1 lb. cut in half	Place beans in 1½-qt. casserole. Add ½ cup water. Cover. Stir beans after 7 minutes.	High (10)	15 to 17	Tenderness in beans varies. Test beans after 15 minutes to determine if more cooking is needed.
Beans Frozen French Cut Green & Wax	10-oz. pkg. (about 2 cups)	Place beans in 1-qt. casserole. Add 2 tablespoons water. Cover.	High (10)	7 to 9	For 2 packages or about 4 cups frozen beans microwave 12 to 15 minutes.
Beans Frozen Lima	10-oz. pkg (about 2 cups)	Place limas in 1-qt. casserole. Add ¼ cup water. Cover.	High (10)	5 to 7	For 2 packages or about 4 cups frozen limas microwave 9 to 11 minutes.
Beets Fresh Whole	1 bunch (5 medium)	Place beets in 2-qt. casserole. Add ½ cup water. Cover.	High (10)	22 to 25	After cooking, skins peel easily. Slice or dice and season.
Broccoli Fresh Spears	1 bunch (1¼ to 1½ lbs.)	In 3-qt. oblong glass baking dish, arrange broccoli spears with stalks to outside of dish and flowerets in center. Add ¼ cup water. Cover with plastic wrap, turning back one corner to vent. Rotate dish ½ turn after 6 minutes.	Medium High (7)	12 to 14	Larger, more mature stalks should be peeled. As an alternate arrangement place in circular dish, flowers to center stalks to edges.
Broccoli Fresh Cut	1 bunch (1¼ to 1½ lbs.) cut into 2 in. pieces	Place broccoli in 2-qt. casserole. Add ½ cup water. Cover.	High (10)	8 to 10	Broccoli cooks most evenly cut in 2-in. pieces.

Vegetable	Amount	Instructions	Power	Time (min.)	Comments
Broccoli Frozen Chopped	10-oz. pkg. (about 2 cups)	Place broccoli in 1-qt. casserole. Add 2 tablespoons water. Cover. Stir after 4 minutes.	High (10)	6 to 8	For 2 packages or about 4 cups frozen broccoli microwave 10 to 12 minutes.
Broccoli Frozen Spears	10-oz. pkg.	Place broccoli in 1-qt. casserole. Add 3 tablespoons water. Cover.	High (10)	6 to 8	
Brussels Sprouts Fresh	1 lb.	Place Brussels sprouts in 1½-qt. casserole. Add ¼ cup water. Cover.	High (10)	6 to 8	Trim dry or old outer leaves and cut extra-large sprouts in half before cooking.
Brussels Sprouts Frozen	10-oz. pkg. (1½ to 2 cups)	Place Brussels sprouts in 1-qt. casserole. Add 2 tablespoons water. Cover. Stir Brussels sprouts after 4 minutes.	High (10)	6 to 8	For 2 packages or about 3 to 4 cups frozen Brussels sprouts microwave 12 to 15 minutes.
Cabbage Fresh Chopped	1 medium head (about 2 lbs.)	Place cabbage in 1½ or 2-qt. casserole.	High (10)	10 to 12	Use large enough casserole so cabbage fits loosely.
Cabbage Fresh Wedges	1 medium head (about 2 lbs.)	Place cabbage in 3-qt. casserole. Add ¼ cup water. Cover.	High (10)	9 to 11	Use large enough casserole so cabbage fits loosely.
Carrots Fresh Whole	1 to 2 lbs.	Place carrots in 1½-qt. casserole. Add ½ cup water. Cover.	High (10)	1 lb.- 12 to 14 2 lbs.- 18 to 20	Size of carrots affects cooking time; larger carrots take longer time.
Carrots Fresh Sliced	1 lb. (6 to 8 carrots)	Place carrots in 1½-qt. casserole. Add ¼ cup water. Cover.	High (10)	9 to 11	Cut slices about ¼-in. thick. Old carrots take longer to cook. Diagonally sliced carrots reduce cooking time by about 2 minutes.
Carrots Frozen Sliced	10-oz. pkg. (about 2 cups)	Place carrots in 1-qt. casserole. Add 2 tablespoons water. Cover.	High (10)	6 to 8	
Cauliflower Fresh Whole	1 medium head (about 1½ lb.)	Place cauliflower in 1½-qt. casserole. Add ½ cup water. Cover.	Medium High (7)	12 to 15	Let stand about 5 minutes before serving. If desired, surround on platter with French style green beans.
Cauliflower Fresh Flowerets	1 medium head (about 1½ lb.) cut into flowerets	Place cauliflower in 1½-qt. casserole. Add ½ cup water. Cover.	High (10)	10 to 12	
Cauliflower Frozen Flowerets	10-oz. pkg. (about 1½ cups)	Place cauliflower in 1-qt. casserole. Add 2 tablespoons water. Cover.	High (10)	6 to 8	For 2 packages or about 3 cups flowerets microwave 12 to 14 minutes.
Celery Fresh	4 cups ½-in. slices	Place celery in 2-qt. casserole. Add ¼ cup water. Cover.	High (10)	11 to 13	Celery is crisp-tender when cooked.

Corn Frozen Kernel	10-oz. pkg. (about 2 cups)	Place corn in 1-qt. casserole. Add 2 tablespoons water. Cover. Stir after 2 minutes.	High (10)	4 to 6	For 2 packages or about 4 cups microwave 8 to 9 minutes.
Corn on the Cob Fresh	1 to 5 ears (see time column)	Place corn in 2 or 3-qt. casserole. If corn is in husk, use no water; if corn has been husked add ¼ cup water. Cover. Rearrange after half of time.	High (10)	2 to 3 per ear	For convenience and freshest flavor, microwave corn in husk.
Corn on the Cob Frozen	1 to 6 ears (see time column)	Place corn in 2-qt. oblong glass baking dish. (No additional water needed.) Cover tightly with lid or plastic wrap. Turn over after half of time. Let stand 5 minutes after microwaving.	High (10)	1 ear: 5 to 6 min. 2 to 4 ears: 3 to 4 min./ear	
Eggplant Fresh	1 medium (about 1 lb.) 4 cups cubed	Place peeled, diced eggplant in 2-qt. casserole. Add 2 tablespoons water. Cover.	High (10)	5 to 6	If peeled, cubed vegetable is prepared ahead of cooking, cover with salted water to retain color and flavor. Let stand 5 minutes.
Mushrooms Fresh Sliced	½ to 1 lb. (see time column)	In 1½-qt. casserole place 2 tablespoons butter or water for each 1 lb. mushrooms. Add mushrooms. Cover. Stir mushrooms after half of time.	High (10)	½-lb.- 2 to 4 1 lb.- 4 to 7	Don't overcook. As soon as color begins to darken remove from oven and let stand a few minutes before serving. If mushrooms are thinly sliced they will take minimum time.
Onions Fresh	4 to 8 medium quartered	Place onions in 1½ to 2-qt. casserole. Add ½ cup water. Cover.	High (10)	4-10 to 12 8-14 to 16	Timing gives tender but not mushy onions.
Okra Frozen Whole	10-oz. pkg.	Place okra in 1-qt. casserole. Add 2 tablespoons water. Cover.	High (10)	7 to 9	
Parsnips Fresh	1 lb. (2 to 3 cups cubed)	Place peeled, cubed parsnips in 1½-qt. casserole. Add ¼ cup water. Cover.	High (10)	10 to 12	Age of parsnips affects microwaving time.
Peas Fresh Shelled	2 lbs.	Place peas in 1-qt. casserole. Add ¼ cup water. Cover. Stir peas after 6 minutes. After microwaving, add 1 tablespoon butter and let stand 5 minutes.	High (10)	10 to 12	Fresh young peas microwave best at High. Mature peas (yellow color, some sprouts) should be microwaved at Low Power for longer time.
Peas Frozen Shelled	10-oz. pkg. (about 2 cups)	Place peas in 1-qt. casserole. Add 2 tablespoons water. Cover. Stir peas after 3 minutes.	High (10)	6 to 7	For 2 packages or about 4 cups microwave 9 to 10 minutes.
Potatoes Fresh Whole Sweet or White	6 to 8-oz. each (see time column)	Pierce with cooking fork. Place on paper towel on floor of microwave oven, 1-in. apart in square shape. Turn potatoes over after half of time.	High (10)*	1-4 to 6 2-6 to 8 3-8 to 12 4-12 to 16 5-16 to 20	*Potatoes may still feel firm when done; let stand to soften. Dry or old potatoes do not microwave well whole. Peel and dice them before microwaving.

*NOTE: When microwaving more than 2 potatoes, moisture can collect in oven. This does not harm food or oven and will evaporate (or may be wiped with cloth) when door is opened. Cook potatoes just until done. Excessive cooking dehydrates them.

NOTE: Not all potatoes are suitable for baking. Dry or old potatoes do not bake well, either conventionally or by microwaving, and are best peeled, cubed and cooked with water.

Potatoes Fresh Cubed White	4 potatoes (6 to 8-oz. each)	Peel potatoes and cut into small pieces (1-in. cubes). Place in 2-qt. casserole with ½ cup water. Cover.	High (10)	12 to 14	Drain potatoes and mash with electric mixer, adding 1 teaspoon salt, ½ cup milk and 2 tablespoons butter.
Spinach Fresh	10 to 16-oz. washed	Place spinach in 2-qt. casserole (no extra water needed). Cover.	High (10)	5 to 7	Water which clings to leaves is enough moisture to create steam for cooking.
Spinach Frozen Chopped & Leaf	10-oz. pkg.	Place spinach in 1-qt. casserole. Add 3 tablespoons water. Cover. Break up and stir well after 4 minutes.	High (10)	6 to 7	
Squash* Fresh Summer Yellow	1 lb. sliced or cubed	Place squash in 1½-qt. casserole. Add ¼ cup water. Cover	High (10)	10 to 12	If desired, add 2 tablespoons butter to water before microwaving.
Squash Fresh Winter (Acorn or Butternut)	1 to 2 squash (about 1 lb. each)	Cut in half and remove fibrous membranes. In 8-in. square dish or 2-qt. oblong glass baking dish, place squash cut side down. Cover with wax paper. Turn cut side up and brush with butter (sprinkle with brown sugar if desired) after 10 minutes.	High (10)	13 to 15	Wax paper cover is best to hold right amount of steam. Let stand 5 minutes.
Squash Frozen Summer	10-oz. pkg. (about 1½ cups)	Place squash in 1-qt. casserole (no extra water needed). Cover.	High (10)	4 to 6	Ice crystals in frozen squash provide enough moisture for microwaving. For 2 packages or about 3 cups microwave 7 to 10 minutes.
Succotash Frozen	10-oz. pkg. (about 2 cups)	Place succotash in 1-qt. casserole. Add 2 tablespoons water. Cover.	High (10)	7 to 9	For 2 packages or 4 cups frozen succotash microwave 10 to 12 minutes.
Turnips Fresh	1 lb. cubed (2 to 3 medium)	Place peeled cubed turnips in 1½-qt. casserole. Add 3 tablespoons water. Cover.	High (10)	10 to 12	If desired, turnips can be mashed with added butter after microwaving.
Vegetables, Mixed Frozen	10-oz. pkg. (about 2 cups)	Place vegetables in 1-qt. casserole. Add 3 tablespoons water. Cover.	High (10)	7 to 9	Lima beans are last vegetable to cook; check them for tenderness. Stir and let stand 5 minutes before serving. For 2 packages or 4 cups frozen mixed vegetables microwave 11 to 13 minutes.
Zucchini* Fresh	1 lb. sliced or cubed	Place zucchini in 1½-qt. casserole. Add ¼ cup water. Cover.	High (10)	9 to 11	If desired, add 2 tablespoons butter to water before microwaving.

*Yellow Squash and Zucchini Combination: In 2-qt. casserole arrange chunks from 1 lb. (4 medium) zucchini and 1 lb. (4 medium) yellow squash. Alternate colors for attractive appearance. Arrange drained strips from 1 jar (2 oz.) pimiento on top. Add 2 tablespoons water; dot with 2 tablespoons butter. Insert temperature probe at center top of casserole, just under top surface. Cover with plastic wrap. arranging loosely around probe to vent. Attach cable end at receptacle. **Microwave at High (10). Set Temp. Set 199°.** When oven signals, let squash stand about 10 minutes. Toss to mix, if desired.
Note: To time cook this casserole. **Microwave at High (10) for 10 to 13 Minutes.**

Scalloped Potatoes

If desired, sprinkle top with paprika and/or ½ cup shredded sharp cheese after cooking. Cheese melts as casserole stands.

POWER LEVEL: High (10)
MICROWAVE TIME: 22½ to 26½ min., total

3 tablespoons butter 2 tablespoons flour 1 teaspoon salt ¼ teaspoon pepper 2 cups milk	Place butter in 1-qt. measuring cup. **Microwave at High (10) ½ Minute**, or until melted. Blend in flour and seasonings. Gradually stir in milk. **Microwave at High (10) 5 to 7 Minutes**, stirring after 3 minutes.
3½ to 4 cups thinly sliced white potatoes (about 3 medium) 2 tablespoons minced onion	Layer half of potatoes, onion and sauce in greased 2-qt. casserole. Repeat layers. Cover.

Microwave at High (10) 17 to 19 Minutes. Remove from oven and let stand 5 minutes before serving.

Makes 4 to 6 servings

Twice Baked Potatoes

POWER LEVEL: High (10)
MICROWAVE TIME: See Recipe

Potatoes	Microwave desired number of potatoes according to chart, page 74. Slice the top from each potato. With teaspoon, remove center of potatoes to mixing bowl, leaving shells intact.
For each potato 2 tablespoons butter 2 tablespoons sour cream ¼ teaspoon salt Dash pepper	Add to mixing bowl butter, sour cream, salt and pepper. Mix with electric mixer until smooth. Divide potato mixture evenly among shells, mounding, if necessary. Sprinkle with chives if desired. Place potatoes on plate suitable for microwave oven. Potatoes may be refrigerated at this point if desired.

If potatoes are microwaved immediately, **Microwave at High (10) 1 Minute** per potato. If more than 2 potatoes are microwaved at one time, arrange in a circle.

If potatoes are microwaved from refrigerator temperature, increase time for each potato by ½ minute.

Eggplant Italiano

This hearty vegetable casserole goes well with plain meats such as roasts, lamb, ham or chicken.

POWER LEVEL: High (10)
MICROWAVE TIME: 15 to 18 min., total

1 medium eggplant	Pare eggplant; slice ⅛-in. thick.
2 cans (8-oz. each) tomato sauce 1 to 2 teaspoons oregano ½ cup shredded sharp cheddar cheese, optional	Spread 2 tablespoons tomato sauce in bottom of 2-qt. casserole. Layer half of eggplant, 1 can tomato sauce, half of oregano and half of sharp cheese. Repeat layers. Cover. **Microwave at High (10) 14 to 16 Minutes.**
1 pkg. (6-oz.) mozzarella cheese, sliced	Add mozzarella cheese. **Microwave at High (10) 1 to 2 Minutes.**

Makes 4 to 6 servings

Zippy Zucchini

Covering the custard mixture during the first 4 to 5 minutes of microwaving helps it to cook evenly and shortens the total time.

POWER LEVEL: High (10) and Medium High (7)
MICROWAVE TIME: 15 to 18 min., total

4 cups zucchini, cut into chunks (2 medium) ½ medium onion, thinly sliced	Place zucchini and onion in 10×6×2-in. dish. Cover with plastic wrap, turning one edge back slightly to vent. **Microwave at High (10) 8 to 10 Minutes.** Drain.
4 eggs, beaten 1½ cups (6-oz.) shredded cheddar cheese 1 jar (2-oz.) pimiento, drained ½ teaspoon salt ⅛ teaspoon pepper	In large bowl mix together eggs, cheese, pimiento, salt and pepper. Add zucchini and onions, stirring well. Grease dish in which vegetables were cooked. Pour mixture into dish and cover with paper towel. **Microwave at Medium High (7) 7 to 8 Minutes,** removing paper towel after 4 minutes, until center is set.

Makes 4 servings

Fresh Tomato Garnish:

In 1½-qt. casserole microwave at High (10) for 2 minutes: 1 tablespoon prepared mustard, 1 tablespoon brown sugar, 2 teaspoons white vinegar and ½ teaspoon seasoned salt. Add 2 cups tomatoes, ½ cup celery, ½ cup green pepper and ¼ cup green onion—all finely chopped. Microwave at High for 2 more minutes. Stir well and refrigerate at least 1 hour before serving.

Vegetable Lasagna

POWER LEVEL: Medium High (7)
MICROWAVE TIME: 21 to 26 min., total

2 cans (8-oz. each) .... In small bowl mix together
tomato sauce tomato sauce, tomato
1 can (6-oz.) tomato paste, mushrooms, onion,
paste oregano, basil, salt and
1 can (4-oz.) sliced garlic powder. Spread
mushrooms, drained ½ cup sauce over bottom
¼ cup onion, finely of 3-qt. oblong glass baking
chopped dish. Mix cottage cheese
2 teaspoons leaf with egg. Over sauce layer
oregano half lasagna noodles laid
1 teaspoon basil lengthwise, with half of
1 teaspoon salt spinach, half of cottage
¼ teaspoon garlic cheese mixture, half of
powder tomato sauce, half of
6 lasagna noodles, mozzarella cheese in dish.
cooked Repeat layers.
1 pkg. (10-oz.) frozen **Microwave at**
chopped spinach, **Medium-High (7) for**
thawed and well **21 to 26 Minutes.**
drained Let stand for 5 minutes
2 cups (16-oz.) small before serving.
curd cottage cheese
2 eggs, beaten
1 pkg. (8-oz.) grated
mozzarella cheese

Makes 6 to 8 servings

Creamy Cauliflower

POWER LEVEL: High (10)
MICROWAVE TIME: 13 to 15 min., total

1 tablespoon .... In 2-qt. casserole, stir to
butter, softened mix butter and flour. Stir in
1 tablespoon flour milk, cheeses, pimiento
½ cup milk and seasonings.
1 cup small curd **Microwave at High**
cottage cheese **(10) 6 Minutes,** until
½ cup shredded cheese melts and mixture
cheddar cheese thickens.
1 tablespoon chopped
pimiento
½ teaspoon salt
½ teaspoon pepper
2 pkgs. (10-oz. each)
frozen cauliflower
thawed and drained

½ cup crushed corn .. Mix cauliflower gently into
flakes sauce and sprinkle top with
½ teaspoon paprika corn flakes mixed with
½ teaspoon dill weed paprika and dill weed.
Microwave at High
(10) 7 to 9 Minutes,
until hot.

Makes 6 servings

Wilted Spinach Salad

POWER LEVEL: High (10)
MICROWAVE TIME: 5 to 6 min., total

3 strips bacon .... With scissors, snip bacon
into 1-in. pieces into 3-qt.
casserole. **Microwave**
at High (10)
3 Minutes, until crisp.
With slotted spoon, remove
bacon to paper towels to
drain.

¼ cup vinegar .... To drippings in casserole
2 teaspoons sugar add vinegar, sugar, salt,
¼ teaspoon salt pepper and tarragon.
⅛ teaspoon pepper **Microwave at High**
⅛ teaspoon crushed **(10) 2 to 3 Minutes** to
dried tarragon boil. Stir in celery and
¼ cup chopped onion.
celery
1 tablespoon sliced
green onion

1 pkg. of fresh .... Gradually add spinach to
spinach leaves, hot dressing, tossing to
torn (about 8 cups coat each piece, just until
total) slightly wilted. Add orange
2 medium oranges, segments and crisp bacon
sectioned, each pieces and toss again
section seeded lightly. Serve immediately.
and cut in half*

Makes 8 to 10 servings

*Or substitute 1 can (11-oz.) Mandarin oranges, drained.

Stir Fry Vegetables

POWER LEVEL: High (10)
MICROWAVE TIME: 13 to 15 min., total

1 tablespoon oil ...... In 3-qt. glass casserole
1 tablespoon butter place oil, butter and onions.
3 medium onions, **Microwave uncovered**
quartered **at High (10) for**
lengthwise **5 Minutes** until hot.

1 medium green ...... Stir in and mix well green
pepper, cut in ¼-in. pepper, cabbage, carrots,
wide strips green onions, broccoli,
3 cups thinly-sliced cauliflower, celery, and pea
cabbage pods. Cover.
1 cup carrots **Microwave at High**
(3 medium) sliced **(10) for 4 Minutes.** Stir
diagonally gently. **Microwave at**
¼ cup sliced **High (10) for 4 to 6**
green onions **Minutes** more.
1 cup broccoli
flowerets
1 cup cauliflower
flowerets
3 stalks celery,
diagonally sliced
1 pkg. (10 oz.) frozen
pea pods, defrosted
and drained

Makes 6 to 8 servings

Popular Green Bean Casserole

POWER LEVEL: High (10)   TEMP: 170°
MICROWAVE TIME: 10 to 12 min., total

3 pkgs. (10-oz. each) frozen French-style green beans defrosted and drained **1 can (10-oz.) cream of mushroom soup** **½ cup milk** **1 jar (2-oz.) chopped pimiento, drained**	Separate beans into 1½-qt. casserole. Mix with canned soup, milk and pimiento to blend well.

Insert temperature probe so tip rests at center top of dish just below the surface. Cover with plastic wrap, arranging loosely around probe to vent. Attach cable end at receptacle. **Microwave at High (10). Set Temp, Set 170°.** When oven signals let stand, covered, about 10 minutes. **Arrange Topping of 1 can (3-oz.) French fried onions** in a ring around edge of dish.

Makes about 8 servings

Cheezy Broccoli

POWER LEVEL: High (10)
MICROWAVE TIME: 14 to 17 min., total

¾ cup packaged precooked (minute) rice **1 can (10¾-oz. each) cream of chicken soup** **1 jar (8-oz.) pasteurized processed cheese food** **⅛ teaspoon pepper**	In 2-qt. casserole combine rice, soup, cheese, pepper. **Microwave at High (10) 2 to 4 Minutes,** until cheese melts and can be blended easily.
¼ cup chopped onion **½ cup chopped celery** **¼ cup water chestnuts, diced** **1 pkg. (10-oz.) frozen chopped broccoli, defrosted and well drained**	To cheese mixture, add onion, celery, water chestnuts and broccoli. Stir thoroughly. Cover. **Microwave at High (10) 12 to 13 Minutes.** Stir. Let stand 5 minutes before serving.

Makes about 6 servings

Hot German Potato Salad

POWER LEVEL: High (10)
MICROWAVE TIME: 21 to 24 min., total

4 medium potatoes	Wash and pierce potatoes through with fork. Place on paper towel in microwave oven. **Microwave at High (10) 10 to 12 Minutes,** until tender. Remove from oven, cool slightly, peel potatoes and cut in ⅛-in. slices.
6 strips bacon	In 2-qt. casserole cut bacon in small pieces. Cover with paper towel. **Microwave at High (10) about 6 Minutes,** until crisp. With slotted spoon remove bacon to paper towels to drain. Set aside.
2 tablespoons flour **¼ cup sugar** **1 teaspoon salt** **½ teaspoon celery seed** **⅛ teaspoon pepper**	Stir flour, sugar and seasonings into bacon fat until smooth. **Microwave at High (10) 1 to 2 Minutes,** until bubbly.
1 cup water **½ cup vinegar**	Add water and vinegar to flour mixture. **Microwave at High (10) 4 Minutes,** until mixture boils and thickens. Remove from oven and stir smooth. Add potatoes and bacon; stir gently so potatoes hold their shape. Cover casserole and let stand until ready to serve.

Makes 4 to 6 servings

Vegetable Medley

POWER LEVEL: High (10)
MICROWAVE TIME: 12 to 15 min., total

1 small head cauliflower (1¼ to 1½-lbs.) **1 bunch broccoli (1¼ to 1½-lbs.) cut into spears** **3 to 4 carrots, diagonally sliced ¼ inch thick**	On 12-in. round glass or ceramic dish place head of cauliflower in center. Cover with plastic wrap. **Microwave at High (10) for 4 to 5 Minutes.** Arrange broccoli and carrots around outside.
½ cup butter, melted **½ teaspoon garlic salt** **¼ teaspoon pepper**	Pour butter over vegetables. Sprinkle with garlic salt and pepper. Cover with plastic wrap turning back one edge to vent. **Microwave at High (10) for 8 to 10 Minutes.** Let stand, covered, 5 minutes. Vegetables should be crisp but tender.

Makes 6 to 8 servings

Quick Breads

Pictured top to bottom: *Cherry Caramel Ring (page 81)*
Cornbread Ring (page 80)
Bran-Nut Muffins (page 80)
Savory Cheese Bread (page 82)

Thick, fluffy muffin batters, like the ones below microwave best. Because they are somewhat rich and sweet, they absorb microwave energy evenly. Muffin mixes, which are usually less rich, should be checked and rotated ½ turn if necessary after half of time.

Both muffin recipes below can be varied by changing the fruits and nuts. For cornmeal muffins, use the muffin techniques with batter from Cornbread Ring.

Fluffy Muffins

POWER LEVEL: Medium High (7)
MICROWAVE TIME: Use chart below.

2 cups unsifted all-purpose flour ½ cup sugar 3 teaspoons baking powder ½ teaspoon salt	In mixing bowl stir flour with sugar, baking powder and salt. Make a well in center of dry mixture.
2 eggs, beaten ½ cup cooking oil ½ cup milk	Combine eggs, oil and milk. Add all at once to dry ingredients and stir just to moisten. Fill paper lined microwave containers ½ full. Cook according to chart below. Muffins are done when toothpick stuck in center comes out clean.

Blueberry Muffins Variation: Fold ½ cup rinsed, well drained blueberries into batter. Top with cinnamon sugar.

Makes 12 large muffins

Bran Nut Muffins

POWER LEVEL: Medium High (7)
MICROWAVE TIME: Use chart below.

1½ cups unsifted all-purpose flour 1 cup sugar 5 teaspoons baking powder 1½ teaspoons salt 2 cups whole bran cereal 1 cup chopped nuts (or raisins)	In large mixing bowl stir together flour, sugar, baking powder, salt, bran and nuts or raisins.
2 eggs 1½ cups milk ½ cup cooking oil	Combine eggs, milk and oil. Stir into dry mixture just until all flour is dampened. Fill paper lined muffin cups ½ full.
¼ cup crushed bran cereal or chopped nuts	Sprinkle muffins with cereal or nuts. **Microwave at Medium High (7),** using chart below.

Makes about 24 muffins

Muffin Cooking Chart

POWER LEVEL: Medium High (7)

Muffins	Time	Comments
1 Muffin	½ to ¾ min.	Use microwave safe muffin container or homemade muffin cups (made by cutting down hot drink cups). Check for doneness at minimum time. Rich, thick batters may take longest time.
2 to 4:	1 to 1¼ min.	
5 to 6:	2 to 2½ min.	

Fluffy Blueberry Muffins

Cornbread Ring

POWER LEVEL: Medium (5)
MICROWAVE TIME: 10 to 12 min., total

1 cup yellow corn meal 1 cup unsifted all-purpose flour 2 tablespoons sugar 4 teaspoons baking powder ½ teaspoon salt	In large mixing bowl, stir together cornmeal, flour, sugar, baking powder and salt.
1 egg 1 cup milk ½ cup cooking oil	Add egg, milk and cooking oil. Beat until smooth, about 1 minute.
1 can (3-oz.) French-fried onions, finely crushed 2 tablespoons Parmesan cheese	Place onions and cheese in well-greased 8-in. ring mold. Tilt to coat all sides. Pour batter into ring mold.

Microwave at Medium (5) for 10 to 12 Minutes until toothpick inserted in center comes out clean. Remove from oven and allow to cool slightly. Turn out on cooling rack or serving plate. Serve warm.

Makes 1 (8-in.) ring

Coffee cakes may be microwaved in a round dish, rather than a ring. The richer, sweeter batter cooks evenly, so there will be no depression in the center. Like other quick breads, coffee cakes do not brown, and need a colorful topping or simple icing to give them a finished appearance.

Everyday Coffee Cake

Biscuit mix recipe.

POWER LEVEL: High (10)
MICROWAVE TIME: 6 to 8 min., total

1½ cups buttermilk biscuit mix ¼ cup sugar	In mixing bowl stir together biscuit mix and sugar.
½ cup milk 1 egg 2 tablespoons cooking oil	Add milk, egg and oil. Beat by hand, mixing well. Pour into greased 8-in. round dish.
⅓ cup buttermilk biscuit mix ⅓ cup brown sugar (packed) 2 tablespoons butter 1 teaspoon cinnamon ¼ cup chopped nuts	Blend biscuit mix, brown sugar, butter and cinnamon until crumbly. Sprinkle over batter and sprinkle with nuts. **Microwave at High (10) 6 to 8 Minutes,** rotating ½ turn after 3 minutes. Cool 15 minutes; drizzle with Fine Glaze. Serve warm.

Fine Glaze: Stir together ¾ cup confectioners sugar and 1 tablespoon milk. From tip of spoon, drizzle glaze over cake in spoke fashion.

Makes 1 (8-in. round) cake

Cherry Caramel Ring

POWER LEVEL: High (10) and Medium High (7)
MICROWAVE TIME: 6½ to 8¾ min., total

¼ cup butter	Place butter in 8-in. round dish. **Microwave at High (10) ½ to ¾ Minute,** until melted.
½ cup brown sugar (packed) 2 tablespoons light corn syrup ½ cup pecan halves ¼ cup maraschino cherries, quartered	Sprinkle sugar over butter and add corn syrup. Stir well with fork. Place drinking glass open-side-up in center of dish. Sprinkle with pecans and cherries.
1 roll (10-oz.) refrigerated buttermilk biscuits	Arrange biscuits over mixture in dish in petal shape, squeezing to fit, if necessary. **Microwave at Medium High (7) 6 to 8 Minutes,** rotating ½ turn after 3 minutes. Remove glass and invert onto serving plate. Let dish stand over rolls a few minutes so remaining syrup in dish may drizzle over rolls. Serve warm.

Makes 1 (8-in.) ring

How to Microwave a Caramel Biscuit Ring

Prepare topping in bottom of improvised tube pan made by placing a drinking glass about 4-in. high or inverted 6-oz. custard cup, in an 8-in. dish. Or, use plastic ring mold designed for microwaving.

Arrange biscuits over topping and around glass center.

After cooking, invert onto a serving plate. The ring has a rich caramel-colored syrup over the top and sides, although the bottoms of the biscuits are not brown.

Breads cooked in the microwave oven do not brown or develop a crust as they do conventionally because there is no hot air in the oven to dry out the surfaces. Microwaved bread raises higher during cooking than conventionally baked bread, because it doe not have a firm crust to prevent it from rising too much. For this reason bread must be microwaved in a larger loaf dish. When properly microwaved, breads look set and dry on top and, when touched, the surface springs back.

Colorfully Topped Savory Cheese Bread, above, created for microwaving contains butter and cheese for richness.

Low shape provides maximum exposure to microwave energy for even cooking.

How to Proof Bread Dough

For regular Basic Bread Dough from scratch:

Step 1. Microwave 3-cups of water in 1-qt. measure at High (10) for 2 to 3 minutes until steaming hot.

Step 2. Place bowl of dough in oven next to water. Cover bowl lightly with towel. **Microwave at Warm (1) for 18 to 20 minutes.**

Step 3. Test for rising by making an indention with fingers; dough should **not** spring back and surface should be dry.

Step 4. Microwave as directed in recipe. Bread will not brown. Check for doneness by touching top lightly until it springs back.

Savory Cheese Bread

POWER LEVEL: Medium (5)
MICROWAVE TIME: 8 to 9 min. per loaf

2¾ cups unsifted . . . . . . **all-purpose flour** **2 tablespoons sugar** **½ teaspoon salt** **½ cup (¼-lb.) butter**	In large mixing bowl place flour, sugar, salt and butter. Cut through mixture with pastry blender until mixture resembles coarse meal.
1 pkg. (¼-oz.) active . . **dry yeast** **¼ cup warm water** **1 cup milk** **1 egg, beaten**	Dissolve yeast in warm water. Add to crumbly mixture along with milk and egg. Beat with spoon until well blended.

1 pkg. (½ of 2¾-oz.
  box) dry onion
  soup mix
 1 cup (4-oz. pkg.)
  shredded cheddar
  cheese
	. . Mix together 2 tablespoons onion soup mix and ¼ cup shredded cheese. Set aside. Add remaining soup mix and cheese to batter. Stir well.

Divide batter evenly between 2 well-greased 8×4×3-in. dishes. Sprinkle loaves with reserved cheese mixture. Cover lightly and let rise in warm place 1½ to 2 hours, just until dough is slightly puffy.

Microwave one loaf at a time. **Microwave at Medium (5) 8 to 9 Minutes.** Carefully remove breads to cooling rack.

Serve warm or cool.

Makes 2 loaves

Desserts

Pictured top to bottom: *Fluffy Marshmallow Fruit Pie (page 86)*
Pineapple Upside Down Cake (page 89)
Basic Butter Cupcakes (page 87) with
  Easy Fudge Frosting (page 87)
Early American Gingerbread (page 89)
  with Lemon Sauce (page 92)

Many fruit recipes are versatile enough to accommodate other fruits for a flavor change. The streuseled apple recipe below microwaves well when pears or peaches are substituted for apples.
The butterscotch bananas may be turned into a tasty pineapple sauce by replacing banana pieces with drained canned pineapple slices or chunks. Instead of orange and maraschino cherries in the filled pineapple, try snipped dried apricots and bing cherries for a tart-sweet effect.

Fruit Filled Pineapple

Streuseled Apples

POWER LEVEL: High (10)
MICROWAVE TIME: 10 to 12 min., total

6 cups sliced, peeled apples **¾ cup brown sugar (packed)**	In 8-in. baking dish combine apples and sugar.
½ cup unsifted all-purpose flour **⅓ cup brown sugar (packed)** **⅓ cup quick-cooking oats** **¼ cup butter** **½ teaspoon cinnamon**	With pastry blender mix flour, sugar, oats, butter and cinnamon until crumbly. Sprinkle over top of apples.

Microwave at High (10) 10 to 12 Minutes. Let stand a few minutes before serving.

Makes 6 to 8 servings

Butterscotch Bananas

POWER LEVEL: High (10)
MICROWAVE TIME: 4 to 6 min., total

½ cup brown sugar (packed) **¼ cup rum** **¼ cup butter**	In 1½-qt. casserole stir together brown sugar and rum. Add butter. Cover. **Microwave at High 3 to 4 Minutes,** until sugar is dissolved.
2 large ripe, firm bananas	Cut bananas lengthwise, then crosswise so there are 8 pieces. Add to syrup, stirring to coat each piece. **Microwave at High 1 to 2 Minutes,** until hot. Serve over ice cream.

Makes 4 servings

Fruit-Filled Pineapple

POWER LEVEL: High (10)
MICROWAVE TIME: 11¼ to 13¼ min., total

1 medium fresh pineapple	Cut pineapple, including leafy crown, in half lengthwise. Cut out fruit, leaving outside shell intact. Remove woody core; cut remaining fruit in chunks.
1 cup (3 to 4-oz.) shredded coconut **½ cup toasted sliced almonds** **1 can (11-oz.) mandarin orange sections, drained** **½ cup maraschino cherries without stems, drained** **½ cup sweet orange marmalade**	Toss pineapple chunks with coconut, almonds, oranges, cherries and marmalade. Place pineapple shells in 3-qt. oblong glass baking dish or on serving plate suitable for microwave oven. Fill shells with fruit mixture. Cover with wax paper. **Microwave at High (10) 11 to 13 Minutes.**
¼ cup light rum	Measure rum into glass measure. **Microwave at High (10) 15 Seconds.** Remove 1 metal tablespoonful. Pour rest of rum over pineapple. Ignite rum in spoon and pour over pineapple to flame.

Makes 6 servings

Basic Pastry Shell

POWER LEVEL: High (10)
MICROWAVE TIME: 3½ to 4½ min., total

1 cup unsifted all-purpose flour	In small bowl place flour and salt. With pastry
1 teaspoon salt	blender cut in shortening, until mixture resembles the
6 tablespoons shortening	size of small peas.
2 tablespoons cold water ..	Sprinkle water over flour-shortening mixture. Stir with fork to form ball.

Roll out on floured pastry cloth with rolling pin to ⅛-in. thickness. Let stand a few minutes before shaping. Use to line 9-in. pie plate shaping pastry to the edge of pie plate. Prick pastry with fork. **Microwave at High (10) 3½ to 4½ Minutes.**

Makes 1 (9-in.) pastry shell

Quiche Pastry

The butter flavor complements quiche. See quiche recipe page 63.

POWER LEVEL: High (10)
MICROWAVE TIME: 4 to 5 min., total

1 cup unsifted all-purpose flour	In small mixing bowl stir together flour and salt. With pastry blender, cut in
½ teaspoon salt	shortening until it has the
3 tablespoons shortening	appearance of cornmeal. Cut in butter until particles
3 tablespoons cold butter	form the size of peas.
2½ tablespoons cold water ..	Sprinkle mixture with cold water. Blend lightly with fingers until dough holds together and can be formed into ball. Roll out to fit 9-in. quiche dish.
1 egg yolk	Brush pastry with mixture
1 teaspoon Worcestershire sauce	of egg yolk and Worcestershire sauce. **Microwave at High (10) 4 to 5 Minutes.** Rotate ½ turn after half of time.

Makes 1 (9-in.) quiche pastry

Crumb crusts complement creamy fillings. A variety of cookie crumbs can vary flavor. Mix ¼ cup melted butter, 1¼ cups crumbs, 2 tablespoons sugar. Press into 9-inch pie plate. Microwave as in chart below.

Adapting Basic Pie and Tart Shells

Weigh down pie shells with rice, or dry beans to prevent crust from puffing.

Check for doneness on bottom of crust. It should look opaque and dry. Top will be dry and blistered.

Tart Shells can be shaped over back of custard cups, or inside cupcake pan. Prick dough thoroughly.

How to Adapt Pies and Tarts

ITEM	TIME/MIN.	POWER LEVEL	COMMENTS
Pie Shells	3½ to 4½	High (10)	Pastry will not brown.
Crumb Crust	1 to 2	High (10)	Use a wet knife for neatest cutting.
Crust from a mix	3½ to 4½	High (10)	Mix and roll out as package directs.
Tarts	2½ to 3½	High (10)	Use basic pastry recipe at above. Loosen cooked pastry immediately after microwaving.

Fluffy Marshmallow Fruit Pie

Pie is creamy and soft when served from refrigerator. For firm pieces which hold sharp cut, serve frozen. Frozen pie releases easily from bottom of pie plate if set on a towel dampened with hot water for a few minutes.

POWER LEVEL: High (10)
MICROWAVE TIME: 2 to 3 min., total

Crumb Pie Shell (see page 85)	Microwave crumb pie shell using the flavor of cookie that best complements filling. Cool.
1 pkg. (10-oz.) large marshmallows **½ cup milk**	In 3-qt. casserole place marshmallows and milk. Cover. **Microwave at High (10) 2 to 3 Minutes,** until mixture can be stirred smooth. Chill in refrigerator (about 30 to 40 minutes) or in pan of ice water, until thickened, stirring occasionally.
1 cup whipping cream, whipped **2 cups fresh fruit**	Fold in whipped cream and peeled and sliced fresh peaches, sliced fresh strawberries or fresh whole raspberries. Pour into crust and decorate with reserved crumbs or additional whipped cream, if desired. Refrigerate several hours or overnight.

Makes 1 (9-in.) pie

Frozen Chocolate Almond Pie

This pie cuts well straight from the freezer. No thawing is necessary. Use wet knife for sharpest cut. Also see tip with above recipe.

POWER LEVEL: High (10)
MICROWAVE TIME: 2 to 3 min., total

Crumb Pie Shell (see page 85)	Microwave crumb pie shell. Cool.
4 milk chocolate candy bars with almonds (1.15-oz. each) **½ of 10-oz. pkg. large marshmallows (about 20)** **½ cup milk**	In 2-qt. casserole place candy, marshmallows and milk. **Microwave at High (10) 2 to 3 Minutes,** until mixture can be stirred smooth. Chill until thickened, stirring occasionally.
1 cup whipping cream, whipped	Fold whipped cream into cooled chocolate mixture. Pile into pie shell and freeze until firm.

Makes 1 (9-in.) pie

Apple Graham Pie

POWER LEVEL: High (10)   Temp. 199°
MICROWAVE TIME: 8 to 10 min., total

½ cup (¼-lb.) butter **¼ cup sugar** **2 cups graham cracker crumbs**	In large glass mixing bowl place butter. **Microwave at High (10) 1 Minute,** until melted. Add sugar and crumbs. Mix well. Press half of mixture firmly and evenly into 9-in. pie plate.
5 cups thinly sliced apples (4 to 6 medium) **½ cup sugar** **1 teaspoon cinnamon**	In large mixing bowl place apple slices; they should be ⅛ to ¼-in. thick. Add sugar and cinnamon, mixing well. Mound and press down into crumb crust.

Cover apples with remaining crumbs to make top crust. Press crumbs down firmly, especially at edges, to prevent boilover.

Insert temperature probe so tip is in center of pie and tip is inserted no more than 1-inch in pie. Cover with wax paper. Attach cable end at receptacle. **Microwave at High (10), Set Temp. Set 199°.** Let stand 10 minutes, then remove paper so topping can crisp. For firmer top surface, pat down during standing time.

Makes 1 (9-in.) pie

Pumpkin Pie

POWER LEVEL: High (10) and Medium (5)
MICROWAVE TIME: 24 to 28 min., total

½ cup (¼-lb.) butter	In 10-in. pie plate place butter. **Microwave at High (10) 1 Minute,** until melted.
2 cups vanilla wafer crumbs **2 tablespoons sugar**	Add crumbs and sugar; mix well. Firmly press on bottom and up sides of dish. **Microwave at High (10) 2 Minutes,** rotating dish ½ turn after 1 minute.
1 can (16-oz.) mashed pumpkin **1 cup brown sugar** **1 tablespoon pumpkin pie spice** **1 tablespoon flour** **½ teaspoon salt** **1 can (12-oz.) evaporated milk** **2 eggs, beaten**	In 2-qt. casserole blend together pumpkin, brown sugar, pumpkin pie spice, flour, salt, evaporated milk and eggs. **Microwave at Medium (5) 7 to 9 Minutes,** stirring every 4 minutes, until hot and thickened. Pour hot filling into prepared pie shell. **Microwave at Medium (5) 14 to 16 Minutes.** Pie is done when edges are set and center is slightly soft. Let stand about 15 to 20 minutes.

Makes 1 (10-in.) pie

Chocolate Beauty Cake

POWER LEVEL: High (10)
MICROWAVE TIME: 6 to 8 min., total

1½ cups unsifted all-purpose flour 1 cup brown sugar (packed) ¼ cup cocoa 1 teaspoon baking soda ½ teaspoon salt ½ cup water	..In mixing bowl stir together flour, sugar, cocoa, soda and salt. Add water and stir to a stiff shiny batter, about 100 strokes.
½ cup water .... ⅓ cup cooking oil 1 tablespoon vinegar ½ teaspoon vanilla extract	Add additional ½ cup water, oil, vinegar and vanilla. Stir until smooth and well blended.

Pour batter into greased 8-in. round cake dish. **Microwave at High (10) 6 to 8 Minutes.** Rotate ½ turn after half of time. Let stand directly on heat-proof counter or wooden board to cool. Finish with favorite frosting.

Makes 1 (8-in. round) cake

Basic Butter Cake

POWER LEVEL: High (10)
MICROWAVE TIME: 8 to 10 min., per layer

2 cups unsifted all-purpose flour .... 2 cups sugar 3 teaspoons baking powder ½ teaspoon salt	In large mixing bowl stir together flour, sugar, baking powder and salt.
1 cup (½-lb.) .... butter, softened 1 cup milk 1½ teaspoons vanilla extract 1 egg	Add butter, milk, vanilla and 1 egg. Beat 2 minutes at lowest speed of mixer, scraping bowl constantly for first ½ minute.
3 eggs	Stop mixer and add remaining eggs. Continue beating at lowest speed, scraping bowl often, 1 more minute. Batter will lock curdled.

Lightly grease two 8-inch dishes. Divide batter between dishes, spread evenly. **Microwave at High (10) 8 to 10 Minutes.** Rotate ¼ turn after 5 minutes. Let stand directly on heat-proof counter or wooden board to cool 15 minutes. Cake may then be turned out on wire rack to complete cooling, if desired.

Makes 2 (8-in. round) cakes

Confectioners Sugar Icing:
In 1½-qt. casserole stir 1-lb. pkg. confectioners sugar, ¼ cup milk, ¼ teaspoon vanilla. Top with ¼ cup sliced butter. Microwave at High (10) 2 minutes. Stir smooth.

Easy Fudge Frosting:
In 1½-qt. casserole stir 1 cup sugar, ¼ cup butter, ¼ cup evaporated milk. Microwave at High (10) 3 to 4 minutes, until bubbly. Blend in 1 cup semi-sweet chocolate chips, 1 cup marshmallow creme and 1 teaspoon vanilla extract.

Chocolate Chip Filled Cupcakes.

Chocolate Chip Filled Cupcakes

Batter from 2-layer chocolate cake mix Chocolate Chip Filling (below)	To make each cupcake, measure about 2 teaspoons batter into paper liner. Cover with 1 tablespoon filling. Top with 2 more teaspoons of batter.

Microwave cup cakes using chart below. As cupcakes cook, filling will form in center.

Chocolate Chip Filling: Stir together 1 pkg. (8-oz.) softened cream cheese, ⅓ cup sugar, 1 egg, ⅛ teaspoon salt, until well mixed. Blend in 1 pkg. (6-oz.) chocolate chips (or 1 cup mini chips).

Makes 30 cupcakes

Cupcake Cooking Chart
POWER LEVEL: **Medium High (7)**

CUPCAKES	TIME MINUTES	COMMENTS
1	½	
2	¾ to 1	Fill paper liners only half full. When cooking several cupcakes, you may notice some will be done before others. If so, remove those that are done and continue cooking the rest a few seconds more.
3	¾ to 1¼	
4	1¼ to 1½	
5	1½ to 2	
6	2 to 2½	

Popular Carrot Cake

POWER LEVEL: High (10)
MICROWAVE TIME: 13 to 15 min., total

1½ cups sugar . . . . **1 cup cooking oil** **1 teaspoon vanilla extract** **3 eggs**	In large mixing bowl blend sugar, oil and vanilla. Add eggs and beat well.
1½ cups unsifted all-purpose flour **¾ teaspoon salt** **1¼ teaspoons baking soda** **2½ teaspoons cinnamon**	. . In small bowl, stir together flour, salt, soda and cinnamon. Add to sugar-egg mixture and mix in.
2¼ cups raw grated carrots **½ cup chopped walnuts**	. . . . Fold in carrots and walnuts. Pour batter into greased 2-qt. oblong glass baking dish.

Microwave at High (10) 13 to 15 Minutes, rotating dish ½ turn after 8 minutes. Let stand directly on heat-proof counter or wooden board to cool. Frost with Cream Cheese Frosting, page 89, if desired.

Makes 1 oblong cake

Honey Drizzle Cake

This recipe won $5,000 in a microwave recipe contest. The syrup is plentiful, and some people prefer to use only half of it to soak into cake.

POWER LEVEL: High (10)
MICROWAVE TIME: 13 to 15 min., total

5 eggs . . . . **¼ cup sugar** **⅛ teaspoon salt**	Separate eggs. In large mixer bowl beat egg whites until foamy. Gradually beat in ¼ cup sugar and salt until fluffy.
½ cup sugar . . . . **1 teaspoon vanilla extract**	In small bowl beat egg yolks, ½ cup sugar and vanilla until thick and pale.
1½ cups chopped pecans **1½ cups fine vanilla wafer crumbs** **1½ teaspoons baking powder** **1 teaspoon cinnamon**	Fold yolk mixture into egg whites thoroughly. Blend pecans, wafer crumbs, baking powder and cinnamon; sprinkle over top. Fold all ingredients together well.

Pour into greased 8-in. square dish. **Microwave at High (10) 5 to 7 Minutes.** Remove cake from oven and cook Honey Syrup (below). Carefully pour ⅔ syrup over cake. Serve in small pieces, warm or cold, with unsweetened whipped cream and remaining syrup.

Honey Syrup: In 1½-qt. casserole stir together ¾ cup water, ¾ cup sugar and ⅓ cup honey. **Microwave at High (10) 6 Minutes,** stirring after 3 minutes.

Makes 1 (8-in.) square cake

Orange-Glazed Fruit Cake

Orange-Glazed Fruit Cake

POWER LEVEL: High (10)
MICROWAVE TIME: 12 to 17 min., total

1 cup (3 to 4-oz.) coconut **1 cup unsifted all-purpose flour** **1½ cups confectioners sugar** **2 teaspoons baking powder**	. . . . . . In mixing bowl stir together coconut, flour, confectioners sugar, and baking powder.
¾ cup butter, melted **3 eggs, beaten** **½ cup milk**	. . Add butter, eggs and milk. Mix well.
2 cups chopped candied fruit **1½ cups chopped pecans**	. . . . . . Stir in fruit and nuts. Pour batter into greased 12 cup plastic fluted tube dish.

Microwave at High (10) 10 to 13 Minutes. Cool 1 hour before inverting onto serving dish. Spoon Orange Glaze over cake.

Orange Glaze: In 1-qt. casserole stir together ½ cup sugar and 1 cup orange juice. Cover. **Microwave at High (10) 2 to 4 Minutes,** until boiling.

Makes 1 (10-in.) cake

Pineapple Upside Down Cake

For variety substitute peaches for pineapple and almond extract for vanilla.

POWER LEVEL: High (10)
MICROWAVE TIME: 8½ to 12 min., total

¼ **cup butter**	In 8-in. round cake dish place butter. **Microwave at High (10) ½ to 1 Minute,** to melt. Sprinkle sugar over butter. Drain pineapple (save liquid) on paper towels and arrange in dish. Decorate with cherries.
⅓ **cup brown sugar (packed)**	
1 **can (8¼-oz.) pineapple slices**	
4 **maraschino or candied cherries, cut in half**	
Batter from 1-layer yellow cake mix, using liquid from pineapple plus milk to total ½ cup.	Carefully spread batter over fruit in dish.
	Microwave at High (10) 8 to 11 Minutes. Some batter may run onto edges of dish, but will not spill. When done, toothpick stuck in cake comes out clean. Invert cake onto plate, let dish stand over cake a few minutes. Serve warm.

Makes 1 (8-in. round) cake

Early American Gingerbread

POWER LEVEL: Medium High (7)
MICROWAVE TIME: 10 to 11 min., total

1½ **cups unsifted all-purpose flour**	In mixing bowl stir together flour, sugar, baking soda, ginger, cinnamon and salt.
½ **cup sugar**	
¾ **teaspoon baking soda**	
½ **teaspoon ginger**	
½ **teaspoon cinnamon**	
½ **teaspoon salt**	
½ **cup soft shortening**	Add shortening, egg, molasses and water. Beat 2 minutes on medium speed of mixer until well blended.
1 **egg**	
½ **cup light molasses**	
½ **cup hottest tap water**	

Pour batter into greased 8-in. round cake dish or 9-in. plastic tube dish. **Microwave at Medium High (7) 10 to 11 Minutes.** Rotate ½ turn after half of time. When cake is done let stand directly on heat-proof counter or wooden board to cool.

Makes 1 (8 or 9-in. round) cake

Basic Cheesecake

Cheesecake, which is a custard rather than a batter, is especially appropriate for microwaving.

POWER LEVEL: High (10) and Medium (5)
MICROWAVE TIME: 16¼ to 21¼ min., total

3 **tablespoons butter**	In 8-in. round cake dish place butter. **Microwave at High (10) ¼ to ¾ Minute,** to melt. Stir in crumbs and sugar. Press mixture on bottom and sides of dish. **Microwave at High (10) 1 to 1½ Minutes,** rotating dish ½ turn after 1 minute, until set.
1 **cup fine crumbs (graham cracker or chocolate cookie)**	
2 **tablespoons sugar**	
4 **eggs**	In blender container place eggs, sugar, cream cheese, vanilla and salt. Blend on high speed 1 minute until smooth. (If mixed with electric mixer, use large mixer bowl and mix at high speed 3 minutes.) Pour over back of spoon into crust.*
1 **cup sugar**	
2 **pkg. (8-oz. each) cream cheese**	
2 **teaspoons vanilla extract**	
¼ **teaspoon salt**	

Microwave at Medium (5) 15 to 18 Minutes, until center is almost set. Refrigerate at least 3 hours before serving. Garnish with Whipped Cream Cheese Topping (below) and chocolate curls, if desired.

Makes 1 (8-in.) cheesecake

*Pouring over spoon prevents crust from breaking.

Whipped Cream Cheese Topping: In small mixer bowl place 1 pkg. (3-oz.) softened cream cheese, ½ cup whipping cream and 2 tablespoons sugar. Beat until fluffy. Serve in dollops or spread over top.

Irish Coffee Cheesecake
Prepare recipe above with Graham Cracker Crust. Omit vanilla, add 1 teaspoon instant coffee powder and ¼ cup Irish mist liqueur to filling.

Creme de Menthe Cheesecake
Prepare recipe above with Chocolate Cookie Crust. Omit vanilla, add ¼ cup green creme de menthe to filling.

Cream Cheese Frosting: In 2-qt. casserole place 1 lb. pkg. confectioners sugar. Place 1 pkg. (8-oz) cream cheese, 6 tablespoons butter and 2 teaspoons vanilla extract over top. Microwave at High (10) for 1 minute, just until ingredients can be beaten together.

Fruit Topped Cake: Prepare 8-in. round cake dish by buttering sides well. Coat sides with finely ground nuts. Line bottom with circle of wax paper; pour in ½ can pie filling, then gently pour 2 cups prepared cake batter over top. Microwave as in chart (cake mix page 16). Invert finished cake.

Chocolate Chip Bars

Chocolate Chip Bars

POWER LEVEL: High (10)
MICROWAVE TIME: 6 to 7 min., total

½ cup (¼-lb.) butter, softened ¾ cup brown sugar (packed) 1 egg 1 tablespoon milk 1 teaspoon vanilla extract	In small mixer bowl cream together butter and sugar, until fluffy. Add egg, milk, and vanilla. Mix well.
1¼ cups unsifted all-purpose flour ½ teaspoon baking powder ⅛ teaspoon salt 1 cup (6-oz.) semi-sweet chocolate chips, divided ½ cup chopped nuts (optional)	Stir together flour, baking powder and salt. Add to creamed mixture. Blend well. Stir in ½ cup chocolate chips and nuts. Spread in greased 8-in. square baking dish. Sprinkle with remaining ½ cup chocolate chips. **Microwave at High (10) 6 to 7 Minutes,** rotating dish ¼ turn after 3 minutes, until done. Cool and cut into bars.

Makes about 24 bars

Basic Brownies

You can microwave brownies from a mix using these same directions.

POWER LEVEL: High (10)
MICROWAVE TIME: 6 to 7 min., total

2 eggs 1 cup sugar ½ teaspoon salt 1 teaspoon vanilla extract	In small bowl at medium speed on mixer, beat together eggs, sugar, salt and vanilla, about 1 minute until light.
½ cup (¼-lb.) butter, melted	Add melted butter. Continue beating until thoroughly blended.
¾ cup unsifted all-purpose flour ½ cup cocoa	Mix in flour and cocoa at low speed.
1 cup chopped nuts	Stir in nuts. Spread evenly in greased 8-in. square baking dish.

Microwave at High (10) 6 to 7 Minutes, rotating dish ¼ turn after 3 minutes. When done, top looks dry and will spring back when lightly touched. Cut when cold.

Makes about 20 brownies

Raspberry Tart Squares

POWER LEVEL: High (10) and Medium High (7)
MICROWAVE TIME: 14½ to 15 min., total

¾ cup butter 1 cup brown sugar 1½ cups unsifted all-purpose flour 1 teaspoon baking powder ½ teaspoon salt 1½ cups quick-cooking oatmeal 1 cup finely chopped pecans	In 2-qt. oblong glass baking dish, place butter. **Microwave at High (10) 1½ to 2 Minutes,** until melted. Stir in brown sugar, flour, baking powder, salt, oatmeal and pecans; blend well. Remove half of crumb mixture to bowl or wax paper. Pat remaining crumbs evenly over bottom of dish. **Microwave at High (10) 4 Minutes,** rotating dish ½ turn after 2 minutes.
1 jar (12-oz.) raspberry jam	Cover patted-out crumbs with raspberry jam and sprinkle with remaining crumbs.

Microwave at Medium High (7) to 9 Minutes, rotating dish ½ turn after 4 minutes. Cool completely before cutting.

Makes about 30 squares

Caramel Popcorn: In 4-qt. dish place 1-lb. box brown sugar, ½ cup butter, ½ cup light corn syrup and 1 tablespoon water. Microwave at High (10) 9 minutes, stirring after 5 minutes. Add 2 teaspoons soda. Pour over 3 quarts popcorn and 1 cup peanuts; toss. Spread on foil to cool or form into balls.

Chocolate Nut Bark: Melt 12-oz. pkg. semi-sweet chocolate chips as shown at right. Stir in 1 cup whole toasted almonds. Spread thinly over wax paper covered cardboard, or cookie sheet. Chill until firm. Break into pieces.

Chocolate Chips: Cover dish of chips with plastic wrap and Microwave at Medium (5). For 6-oz. pkg. (1 cup) Microwave 2½ minutes until chips are glossy but hold their shape. For 12 oz. pkg., Microwave 4 minutes.

Munching Peanut Brittle

This is the same old-fashioned recipe which required constant stirring in a black iron skillet. Stir only 2 times when microwaving.

POWER LEVEL: High (10)
MICROWAVE TIME: 7 to 9 min., total

1 cup sugar . . . . In 1½-qt. casserole stir
½ cup white corn together sugar and syrup.
syrup **Microwave at High (10) 3 Minutes.**

1 cup roasted, ... Stir in peanuts.
salted peanuts **Microwave at High (10) 3 to 4 Minutes,** until light brown.

1 teaspoon butter . . . . Add butter and vanilla to
1 teaspoon vanilla syrup, blending well.
extract **Microwave at High (10) 1 to 2 Minutes** more. Peanuts will be lightly browned and syrup very hot.

1 teaspoon baking . . . . Add baking soda and
soda gently stir until light and foamy.

Pour mixture onto lightly greased cookie sheet, or unbuttered non-stick coated cookie sheet. Let cool ½ to 1 hour. When cool, break into small pieces and store in air-tight container.

Makes about 1 pound

Almond Brittle

Substitute 1 jar (7-oz.) dry roasted almonds for peanuts and 1 teaspoon almond extract for vanilla. Omit butter and add 1 cup (4-oz.) shredded coconut.

French-Style Fudge

POWER LEVEL: High (10)
MICROWAVE TIME: 7 to 8 min., total

1 can (5-oz.) . . . . In large glass mixing bowl
evaporated milk thoroughly combine milk
2¼ cups sugar and sugar. **Microwave at High (10) 7 to 8 Minutes,** until sugar is dissolved, stirring after 4 minutes.

½ cup butter . . . . Add butter, vanilla,
2 tablespoons vanilla walnuts, semi-sweet
extract chocolate chips and milk
1½ cups chopped chocolate chips to hot milk
walnuts mixture. Stir until
1 package (6-oz.) completely blended. Pour
semi-sweet into buttered 3-qt. oblong
chocolate chips glass baking dish and
1 package (12-oz.) refrigerate until firm.
milk chocolate chips

Makes about 2 pounds

2-Minute Fudge

POWER LEVEL: High (10)
MICROWAVE TIME: 2 min., total

1 box (1-lb.) . . . . In 1½-qt. casserole stir
confectioners sugar, cocoa, salt, milk and
sugar vanilla together until
½ cup cocoa partially blended (mixture is
¼ teaspoon salt too stiff to thoroughly blend
¼ cup milk in all of dry ingredients).
1 tablespoon vanilla Put butter over top in
extract center of dish.
½ cup (¼-lb.) butter **Microwave at High (10) 2 Minutes,** or until milk feels warm on bottom of dish. Stir vigorously until smooth. If all butter has not melted in cooking, it will as mixture is stirred.

1 cup chopped nuts . . Blend in nuts. Pour into well buttered, 8×4×3-in. dish. Chill 1 hour in refrigerator or 20 to 30 minutes in freezer. Cut into squares.

Makes about 36 squares

Scrumptious Butterscotch Sauce

POWER LEVEL: High (10)
MICROWAVE TIME: 3 to 4 min., total

1 tablespoon cornstarch	In 2-qt. casserole stir together cornstarch and brown sugar. Stir in half & half, corn syrup and salt. Add butter. Cover. **Microwave at High (10) 3 to 4 Minutes,** stirring after 2 minutes, until thickened and sugar is dissolved.
1¼ cups light brown sugar (packed)	
½ cup dairy half & half	
2 tablespoons light corn syrup	
⅛ teaspoon salt	
¼ cup butter	
1 teaspoon vanilla extract	Add vanilla and stir until smooth and well blended. Let stand 5 minutes. Serve warm or cold.

Makes 1½ cups

Cinnamon Sugar Sauce

POWER LEVEL: High (10)
MICROWAVE TIME: 2½ to 3 min., total

½ cup sugar	In 1-qt. casserole stir together sugar, cornstarch, cinnamon and water, until completely smooth. Cover. **Microwave at High (10) 2½ to 3 Minutes,** stirring sauce after 1 minute.
1½ tablespoons cornstarch	
1 teaspoon cinnamon	
1 cup hot tap water	
2 tablespoons butter	Stir in butter until well blended. Serve warm.

Makes 1⅓ cups

Lemon Sauce

Prepare recipe for Cinnamon Sugar Sauce, omitting cinnamon. Stir 1 tablespoon lemon juice and 1 to 2 teaspoons finely grated lemon peel into sugar mixture.

Cherries Jubilee: In 2-qt. casserole combine ¾ cup sugar and 3 tablespoons cornstarch. Drain cherries and gradually add juice to sugar mixture along with 1 teaspoon grated lemon peel. Microwave at High (10) 4 to 6 minutes. Add cherries.

Marshmallow Cream Sauce: In 2-qt. casserole add 2 tablespoons milk to 2 jars (7-oz. each) marshmallow creme. Microwave at Medium (5) for 2 to 3 minutes. Stir well.

Mint Sauce: Place 1 package (7¼-oz.) chocolate-covered mint patties in 1-qt. glass measure with ¼ cup whipping cream. Microwave at Medium (5) for 2 to 2½ minutes. Stir until smooth.

Toasted Coconut: Spread 1 cup coconut (4-oz. can) in thin layer in glass pie plate. Microwave at High (10) for 3 to 5 minutes, stirring every minute. Serve over pie, pudding, or frosted cake.

Dessert Fondue: Prepare Fudge Sauce or Butterscotch; thin with brandy, rum or liqueur if desired. Pour into fondue pot. Use banana slices, maraschino cherries, pineapple chunks and other fruits, or angel food or pound cake pieces for dipping.

Fudge Sauce: In 3-qt. casserole mix 1 cup sugar, ¼ teaspoon salt and 1 can (5-oz.) evaporated milk. Microwave at High (10) for 4 to 6 minutes until boiling, stirring after 3 minutes. Stir in 2 squares (2-oz.) unsweetened chocolate until melted. Add 2 tablespoons butter and 1 teaspoon vanilla extract.

Printed in Japan
(4420AG) 92. 10. ⑩